"This book is a very interesting and readable chronicle of an African American person growing up in the '60s in the segregated South. Having grown up in Mississippi and having spent some time pursuing the legal profession in Baton Rouge, at Southern, I can relate to many of the experiences chronicled by Judge Pitcher. I applaud Judge Pitcher for recording, for those who may follow in his footsteps, his stellar experience as a lawyer, a judge, and a law school administrator. It is a good read for aspiring lawyers and enlightening for those interested in the law and the history of the era, and the geographic area, that he describes."
—HON. REUBEN V. ANDERSON, former Mississippi Supreme Court justice

"Judge Freddie Pitcher Jr., chancellor emeritus of the Southern University Law Center, continues to break barriers beyond the classroom and the bench. In his memoir, Pitcher gives the reader a closer glimpse into the challenging journey from Valley Park that has made him the thought leader and inspiration he is today. I, along with the Southern University Law Center community, salute him for his leadership, wisdom, and philanthropic contributions toward molding and empowering the next generation of legal professionals. He has been a trailblazer all his life, and his memoir chronicles a transformative life and career."
—JOHN A. PIERRE, chancellor and professor of law, Southern University Law Center

# BREAKING
## BARRIERS

# BREAKING BARRIERS

## A VIEW FROM THE BENCH

JUDGE FREDDIE PITCHER JR.

LOUISIANA STATE UNIVERSITY PRESS

BATON ROUGE

Published by Louisiana State University Press
lsupress.org

DESIGNER: *Mandy McDonald Scallan*
TYPEFACE: *Minion Pro*

Jacket photograph: Judge Pitcher's official First Circuit Court of Appeal portrait. Don Boyne Photography Studio, Houma, LA.

Unless otherwise noted, all photographs are from the author's family collection.

Cataloging-in-Publication Data are available from the Library of Congress.
ISBN 978-0-8071-7811-9 (cloth: alk. paper) — ISBN 978-0-8071-7810-2 (pdf) — ISBN 978-0-8071-7812-6 (epub)

*In memory of my parents,*
*the late Freddie Pitcher Sr. and Lucy Angrum Pitcher,*
*who laid the foundation for my educational,*
*spiritual, and moral development,*
*inspiring me to strive to achieve a better life for myself,*
*my family, and my community*

# CONTENTS

# FOREWORD

Freddie Pitcher Jr. dared to pursue a career as a lawyer during a time when most of the boys who shared the bench at the corner store in the "hood" would have been happy to pursue a blue-collar job at one of the local plants. Although wanting Freddie to be successful at whatever profession he chose, Freddie's parents were not at all keen on him becoming a lawyer.

However, motivated by his inner passion for the legal profession and the influence of a close relative, he decided to think outside the box and study law. After graduating from law school, passing the state bar exam, and proving that he could make a good living from his law practice, he had the audacity to seek a judgeship, a success that had never been achieved by a Black person in Baton Rouge, Louisiana, where he lived. A Black man in a city and state with a history and culture of race-line voting who lacked a traditional family pedigree of lawyers, he forged headlong into a campaign against a white opponent, seeking election to the Baton Rouge City Court. Demographically the race was not in his favor. Never in the history of Baton Rouge or East Baton Rouge Parish had a Black person been elected to a position when running head-to-head against a white candidate. Many believed that the time had not yet come for this to happen. The prevailing sentiment in the community was that a Black candidate could run but couldn't win. To the amazement of many, Freddie Pitcher was not only elected the first Black city court judge, but he was subsequently elected the first Black district court judge and the first Black appellate court judge in the history of East Baton Rouge Parish, Louisiana.

This story is not only about his destination but also about his journey, a journey that would take all of the faith, intestinal fortitude, prayers, hard work, and unexpected help from nontraditional sources to achieve his ultimate success. These things took him from the bench of the neighborhood store to the judicial bench as a judge and chancellor of a law school, which was a genuinely transformative experience for him, his family, and the entire community.

*Thomas J. Durant Jr.*
Emeritus Professor
Department of Sociology & African American Studies
Louisiana State University
Baton Rouge

# BREAKING
## BARRIERS

# Election Night

### *A Night of Anxiety and Jubilation*

A T 6:00 P.M., it began to get dark. The polls would close in two hours. I had done all that I could do by this point, so I made my way to clean up, get my wife, Harriet, and our eleven-year-old daughter, Kyla Dean, and head to the hotel to await the election returns.

It had been an exciting but roller-coaster day. After riding out an early-morning rainstorm full of thunder and lighting, Louis Hamilton and I drove back and forth all over the city, checking on voter turnout at key voting precincts. My campaign's political consultant, David Roach, had crunched the numbers provided by our poll watchers and assured me that we had this election "in the bag." Our get-out-the-vote effort appeared to be working. Now we had to wait for confirmation of David's encouraging precinct analysis. I told Harriet and Kyla Dean that it looked like I would win the city court judgeship. Excited, we headed off to meet my supporters, hopeful that I would be the one to crack the white judicial glass ceiling in Baton Rouge.

Upon arriving at the hotel, we went directly to our suite to await the returns. The polls closed at 8:00 p.m., and, despite David's optimistic prediction, an evening of grueling anxiety lay ahead. Joining us in the suite were members of my campaign team: Dr. Press Robinson, my campaign manager; Charles "Chick" Moore, co-campaign manager; Leroy Kolter; David Roach; Mazie Roberson and her husband, Lon; Rosemary

Alexander; my brother Larry and his wife, Janice; and my sister, Juanita, and her husband, Russell. Others wandered in and out as the evening progressed, many of whom cautioned me not to take a win for granted.

As the votes rolled in, I fell behind immediately. Though the early returns showed that I had made some headway in the city's predominantly white precincts, it was still an open question as to whether 15 percent of Baton Rouge's white voters would place a Black judge on the bench in 1983. My opponent, Bill Weatherford, who, like me, was a former assistant district attorney and attorney general, had a commanding lead, and my family, my supporters, and I began to wonder if David's calculations had been overly optimistic. Kyla asked me if I was losing. Despite my assurances to the contrary, she could not keep from crying. Since most of the Black precincts had yet to report, the agonizing wait continued. Once those totals began to roll in, however, my opponent's lead started to shrink. Cautious optimism filled the room. More than 20 percent of the return still had to be tabulated.

My victory hinged on a big turnout in the precinct politicians called "Big Bertha"—the precinct for voters who lived on the alphabet streets "Avenues A thru K," and their cross streets behind the Southern University campus. Politicians knew residents from the area could provide a substantial number of votes if a candidate successfully got them to the polls.

I flashed back to 4:00 p.m. on election afternoon, when it appeared that Big Bertha's voter turnout was lagging. Canvassers from our campaign headed out to find out the cause. The Avenues had recently been annexed into the city limits, but many of the residents revealed that they didn't realize they were eligible to vote in the current election. My team quickly assembled a caravan of about twenty cars led by Rev. Don Avery to go into the Avenues and ignite the people to get out and vote. Some of our volunteers used megaphones to encourage registered voters to head to the polls, which were still open. Others walked through the neighborhood knocking on doors and passing out my campaign literature. Eventually, lines began to form at the polls as citizens responded to my team's last-ditch efforts.

As predicted, once returns from Big Bertha came in, the last precinct out of a total of ninety-five, I not only caught up with my opponent but surged ahead of him. My family and I were elated. It appeared that my candidacy would prevail, even though the local demographics were not in my favor. I garnered 57 percent of the total vote to Bill Weatherford's 43 percent. In the end, I won 23 percent of the white vote, when my target number was 15 percent. Before heading down to the hotel ballroom to greet my supporters and celebrate this historic victory with them, those of us in the suite upstairs gathered in a prayer of thanks led by Rev. Louis Hamilton.

Having stayed in the suite all evening, I had no idea what awaited me in the hotel ballroom. Much to my surprise, I was greeted by a tremendous crowd of well-wishers, reporters, and television cameras. Someone grabbed my arm and rushed me through the crowd over to the press, abruptly separating me from my wife and daughter. It was not until that moment that I realized my historic victory came at a cost I had not considered: the loss of my personal privacy. Renowned civil rights activist and Georgia state senator Julian Bond, chairman of the NAACP, was also in the ballroom that night celebrating my victory. I remember having my picture taken with him. When that photo later appeared in *Jet* magazine, I began to really understand that my life would never be the same.

The assembled crowd was electric that night and quite exhilarating. I was also exhausted and happy to get home after all of the excitement. As I sat in reflection, I was somewhat astonished to realize that I was the first Black candidate to be elected to a judgeship in Louisiana's capital city. I asked myself how it happened that a kid who grew up in the segregated subdivision of Valley Park in the 1950s and 1960s could rise to such heights in 1983.

# 1

## How It All Began

**M**Y JOURNEY TOWARD a career in the law and the judiciary began in the mid-1940s in Valley Park, an African American community situated in what was then the southern tip of Baton Rouge, Louisiana, a racially segregated city. I was the second child of five children born to Freddie and Lucy Angrum Pitcher. My parents were working-class, as were the majority of Valley Park residents. Although our community's family incomes were relatively low, many residents owned their own homes. Many were skilled craftsmen. Our neighbors were painters, carpenters, bricklayers, roofers, mechanics, laborers, teachers, and preachers.

Valley Park's growth resulted from a lot of families relocating from Mississippi and St. Francisville, Louisiana, a town just north of Baton Rouge. Valley Park back then was a family-based community similar to the proverbial African village. Families looked out for one another. There was hardly anything kids could do without some adult saying, "I am going to tell your mother or father." That threat alone usually kept most of us in check. You would often see family members and friends come together to help build or add on to a house. The community was pretty self-contained. We had barber shops, grocery stores, Superb Laundry and Cleaners, a mechanic's shop, two saloons sitting next to each other, and at least five churches.

The most notable thing about the Valley Park community when I was a child was the city dump. It sat right in the middle of the neighborhood and separated the area developed as Valley Park and a later development known as the Balis subdivision. People generally considered them to be the same community, with the Balis identity merging into Valley Park. The dump dated back to the 1940s.

Valley Street was the primary street in Valley Park. It ran from Perkins Road on the west to Wells Street on the east. Balis Drive, where I lived and grew up, also ran from Perkins Road on the west to Wells Street on the east. Both Valley Street and Balis Drive were about two-and-a-half miles long. The landmass between Valley Street and Balis was the location of the dump. The western section, consisting of high mounds of rotting garbage, could be accessed from Perkins Road to Valley Street to Nairn Street, which led to the dump. Bawell and Wells Streets ran north to south and connected the Balis side of the community to the Valley Park community. Neither street directly connected our neighborhood with surrounding white neighborhoods. You could only enter and leave our community via Valley Street or Balis Street. College Drive, which was not a fully paved street back then, ran from Perkins Road on the west toward Bawell Street on the east, creating a later means of ingress and egress from the neighborhood.

Towards the eastern end of Nairn Street was a two-story incinerator building that continuously burned trash. Its horrific smells exacerbated the foul smell of decay from the mounds of garbage dumped there daily. Plumes of ash from the incinerator's smokestack would escape into the air across the neighborhood. Then the city located a dog pound next to the dump. This unwelcome addition further intensified the foul air quality that the residents of my community endured. Summers were especially harsh because none of the houses had air-conditioning at the time and primarily relied on open windows to get a cool breeze for relief from the heat. Depending on the wind direction, your house could get a good whiff of rotting garbage.

When I started at McKinley Junior High School, I remember how the kids from South Baton Rouge would tease us about the dump and make gestures as if we carried the landfill's smell in our clothes. Fights broke out whenever the teasing got out of hand.

The local government annexed our neighborhood into the city in 1959. The landfill moved to property nearer Lee High School to accommodate construction of the interstate highway that cuts through our neighborhood and splits it in half. The two-story incinerator building that often contributed to those horrific odors was remodeled and became a community recreation center. The residents did not readily accept this transformation, fearful that the center was unhealthy because of the possible contamination from all the trash and garbage dumped there. The land was declared a Superfund site and received extensive remediation before a school and playground were built on it, but questions persist today as to the site's safety.

## School Days

My mother enrolled me in the first grade at Perkins Road Elementary when I was five years old. She first tried to enroll me in the one-room school of Reverend Davis's church but was told I had to be six years old. The school had two teachers, Mrs. Williams and Mrs. Poydras, who taught first through third grades. When my mother produced my birth certificate showing I was only five years old, Mrs. Williams refused to let me in school. My mother argued that I knew my ABCs and would be six years old in April of the following year. Her plea didn't move Mrs. Williams, and I had to leave school after only a few days in attendance.

As fate and luck would have it, my mother's sister Evelina knew the Perkins Road Elementary principal as both were Shiloh Missionary Baptist Church members. She relayed my mother's attempt to get me into school to the principal at Perkins Elementary, who encouraged my mother to stop by. She did, and I was enrolled in the first grade there though I was only five years old. I took a bus to school every morning.

A new elementary school was being built in the Valley Park community at the time. It opened at the beginning of the second semester of that academic year. The school had six classrooms with a cafeteria, an office for the principal, and a secretary. Right next to the classroom complex was a regulation-size basketball court with an asphalt surface. Although the school was new, I can't say that about the textbooks we were given. I remember receiving books with covers that fell off or had no room to write your name.

The principal, Mr. Frederick Piper, was a heavy-set man with a loud, booming voice. When he spoke, the students came to attention. Mr. Piper walked the breezeway holding a board with holes drilled in it to spank recalcitrant students when asked by the teachers to do so. He would slap the board against his own leg to let you know what was in store for you if you got out of line.

The most feared teacher at the whole school was probably Mrs. Inez Chrisentery. She was a taskmaster and a strict disciplinarian. I was in her class for both the third and sixth grades. I recall getting a spanking from her for not having homework or talking in class, and I would get a second one at home if she informed my mother. Mrs. Chrisentery's word was gospel at my house, and she knew it. She became a client years later, after I was admitted to the practice of law, and she was present at the investiture for my first judgeship.

But it was Mrs. Godfrey, my fourth-grade teacher, who gave me the foundation that I built on as I moved up in grade level and life. She taught me phonics, which significantly improved my word pronunciation, spelling, and ability to read. Thanks to her, I started to enjoy reading, which also brought a new zest for knowledge.

My move from elementary to junior high was rather unremarkable. I tried out for the band on a borrowed alto saxophone. I learned to play "Blueberry Hill" by Fats Domino, but nothing else. I didn't practice and therefore didn't make the band. What I wanted to do was to play on the varsity football team like my brother Floyd. You could find me in every sandlot football game around the school and the neighborhood until I broke my arm and dislocated my shoulder. I remember asking Coach Mencer about spring football practice while I had the cast on my arm. He laughed and said: "You already have one broken arm. Why are you asking about spring football?"

In the seventh, eighth, and ninth grades I started hanging out with the wrong crowd. I cut class and walked to Valley Park down the railroad tracks with my friends Henry and Mason. Both Henry and Mason failed the ninth grade while I passed to the tenth. Even though I skipped classes from time to time, I generally kept up with my homework, and failing grades were not something my parents would tolerate. My misadventure with Henry and Mason and their failure was a wake-up call for me. I knew that I was on the wrong path and needed to change course on whom I associated with.

I soon learned the people you hang out with can determine the heights you reach in life, or drag you in the opposite direction. I started hanging out with Fulton Toaston, who also lived in Valley Park. Fulton became my best friend, and he graduated valedictorian of our high school class. His homeroom was full of kids who were excellent students and his friends. His friends became my friends, and I gradually assimilated into being an achiever like them.

I had an altogether different perspective in my last three years in high school. I went from being an average student to an above-average student. I was elected president of my homeroom class, which put me on the student council. I took a speech and drama course and played the role of a janitor in a play that won a competition among the Black high schools in Baton Rouge. I spoke only one line in the entire play. I walked onstage with a bucket and mop and said, very dramatically, "The flowers are growing." I then turned around and walked offstage. Small part, but great experience! I got the chance to travel to Grambling State University to say that one line. Mrs. Mildred West, our speech and drama teacher, and a neighbor who lived a few houses down and across the street from me in Valley Park, was a great motivator and constantly encouraged me to get involved in more than sports. She insisted that her speech and drama class would benefit me greatly if I planned to pursue a career in law. I can genuinely say that she was correct. It was the beginning of my developing confidence in my public speaking, which I have had to do a lot of throughout my adult life. However, my secondary reason for taking her class was that I would be in the midst of many good-looking girls.

I was selected to attend Bayou Boys State during the summer leading up to my senior year in high school. Boys State was a leadership development program for Black boys and a great introduction to the operations of local and state governments. Dennis Stewart, who was from Valley

Park and had attended McKinley, was a counselor for the program and taught me how to operate within the political framework of Boys State. I was district attorney for my parish, then elected to the court of appeal. How prophetic!

After Bayou Boys State and the start of football practice for the 1961–62 season, Head Coach Carl Ford appointed me co-captain of the team. It was indeed an unexpected honor. My co-captain was E. J. Mencer, who graduated as the salutatorian of our senior class. After high school and college, he went on to medical school and became a surgeon.

I don't remember our high school guidance counselors providing much help with career choices. They didn't encourage us to think outside of the box or inspire us to do more incredible things than they thought were possible. Had I told a counselor back then that I wanted to become a judge, I wouldn't have gotten much encouragement. There was only a handful of Black judges in the entire country in 1961 and none in Louisiana. Nowadays, I often have young Black students tell me that they aspire to a judgeship. I tell them that the road to a judgeship starts with preparation, which means they should strive to be the best student, then the best lawyer they can be. If they follow this prescription, reaching their goal will be well within the realm of possibility. I recall that on one career day during my senior year in high school at McKinley, I had gone down to the classroom to meet with a Black attorney scheduled to speak on the law when a teacher came and ushered me out of the room to where a football coach was speaking. I had been co-captain of the football team and made pretty good grades. Yet this teacher had a very limited view of my career prospects, implying that my best bet was to become a physical education teacher and football coach. Sadly, many of my fellow high school classmates suffered the same low expectations. I got into a scuffle with another student in the cafeteria during the last semester of my senior year because the student took food off my plate when he thought I wasn't looking. Our verbal altercation escalated to a few punches, followed by a wrestling match that overturned a few tables. We both ended up before the disciplinary committee. Thankfully, it dawned on one of the teachers on the committee during that proceeding that I was more than just a football player.

I was told that Ms. Marguerite Bayham, chairperson of the disciplinary committee, argued very strongly against my expulsion. She informed the other members of the committee that "it would be a travesty to put this young man out of school with such an excellent academic record." Ms. Bayham's recommendation carried the day, and the committee voted for cafeteria cleanup duty instead of expulsion. My homeroom teacher, Mrs. Cooper, suggested that I write Ms. Bayham a thank-you note, which I happily did.

The assistant principal, Mr. J. D. Young, stopped me in the hallway a few days after the committee meeting and said he had no idea that I was doing as well in school as my transcript indicated. Had he known, he would have pushed me harder, as he felt I could have done even better. Mr. Young's early opinion of me, I am sure, was influenced by his confrontations with my brother Floyd, who he threw out of school in the twelfth grade. He would have been ready to visit the same fate upon me had it not been for Ms. Bayham. The teacher who led me away from meeting with the attorney on career day became a client of mine years later.

My parents were strivers and served as excellent examples for me. Neither my mother nor father graduated from high school. At times, my mother would lament not finishing high school when she had only a year left to go. The last grade of high school in those years was the eleventh grade. My mother had to drop out of school in the tenth grade because she had to move back to her parents' home on Essen Lane, which was quite rural at that time and didn't have transportation to get to and from McKinley, the only Black high school in the parish. During her first few years of high school, she lived with her oldest brother, Steve, and his wife. Her relationship with her sister-in-law deteriorated to the point that she needed to return to her parents' home. She married my father, started having children, and missed that last year of high school. She always wanted more than to be a maid in white folks' kitchens. She convinced my father that she could become a beautician and eventually enrolled at the Capital Area Trade and Vocational School in its cosmetology training program.

The trade school was adjacent to McKinley Junior and Senior High, which put her right next to me in the junior high and my brother Floyd in the senior high. We got a chance to ride to school with her whenever we missed the bus.

There were times when my mother had to give a shampoo or manicure as a practical exercise for a grade. When she first got started and didn't know anyone at the trade school, she would insist that Floyd or I come over at recess to be her test subjects. Floyd was on the football team, and I aspired to be on it. We had to appear tough, so getting a manicure went against our grain. Given our persistence, she let us off the hook and got her sisters to stand in. My mother was excelling with her training, and they were happy to get their nails and hair done for free.

Mom graduated and opened a beauty shop in a room off the back of the house. Dad added the room in anticipation of her graduation. She quickly developed a thriving business, which impacted the bedroom space I shared with my brothers Floyd, Larry, and Glynn. Juanita, our sister, had a room to herself. Every Saturday morning, just like clockwork, we would be awakened by the smell of the chemicals my mother used when giving her customers hair relaxers or perms. She rarely took early-morning customers during the week.

Mom was exceptionally diligent, and we benefited considerably from her contribution to our household's financial bottom line. Mom's success had a lot to do with her warm and charming personality, which endeared her to her customers.

My father worked at Standard Oil Company, which later became Esso, then Humble Oil, and is now ExxonMobil. By the time he retired, he had spent forty-three years at the refinery. Seeing him come home full of dirt and grime from his days of working as a laborer at the plant dissuaded me from wanting a similar job. Still, I admired his grit. He valued education, having dropped out of school as a youngster to work on a farm. He was fortunate enough to get a job as a laborer with the Baton Rouge Water Company, which led to a better job as a laborer with the Standard Oil Company. My father was an experienced bricklayer. Sometimes he took Floyd and me out on weekend jobs to stack bricks and mix the mortar for him. I liked the money but not the hard work.

While I was in junior high school, my father enrolled in an adult education course. He went to class religiously for a couple of years and increased his education level by several grades. Many a night I watched him sit at the dining room table with his workbooks, studying for a particular class. He always insisted that we do homework, even when we didn't have any. He would say, "If I could work at the plant all day, come home, go to night school, and then take time out to study, surely you can." Dad took and passed the apprentice pipefitter exam. He completed the course, became a certified pipefitter, and received a hefty pay increase. Even that achievement was not enough to change my mind about working at the plant. I still wanted to become a lawyer.

## Owens Grocery and the Bench

The Owens Grocery and Market, owned by Mr. Dave and Mrs. Emma Owens, had been a staple in the Valley Park community since 1938 and sat diagonally across the street from our house. We didn't have an official playground or recreation center in Valley Park until I was about fifteen years old. Owens Grocery was where the neighborhood boys would gather to organize pickup games of basketball, football, or softball and go for refreshments after the sports. We bought cold drinks, Dixie cups, cookies, and candy before and after our games. There were two benches in front of the store separated by the entrance. The benches turned out to be an excellent site for camaraderie and companionship for the neighborhood kids.

When I was about five or six years old, I would stand in our front yard and watch the older boys gather in front of the store, desperately wanting to run across the street and join them. One day I was almost hit by a car trying to cross the street to be with them. My brother Floyd, who was five years older, would often chase me back home, insisting that I was too young to hang out with his friends. I often heard them laughing out loud and playing around in front of the store, and I wanted to know what was going on. Floyd and the other guys got tired of running me off, so I became an honorary big boy and would follow them around.

After school and most definitely during the summer months, Owens

Grocery was the spot where we all met. A seating hierarchy existed, with the older boys having priority seating on the benches. The younger boys stood around and listened to them spin wild tales full of fabrications and exaggerations. Their primary topics of conversation were sports and girls. As the older boys graduated or moved on, the kids next up in age got the chance to sit on the Owens Grocery store's bench. When I achieved bench privileges, I, too, engaged in the conversations of the day. The tradition continued with my brother Larry, who was four years younger, and my brother Glynn, who was six years behind Larry.

Mr. Dave and Mrs. Emma laid down three rules that applied to everyone: "no fighting, no cursing, and no interference with the coming and going of customers to the grocery." Violate the rules, and you lose your "bench and store privileges." Serious infractions would result in a face-to-face confrontation and tongue lashing from Mrs. Emma. She stood only about five feet tall, but you would think she was at least seven feet tall when she laid into you after a rule violation. After you apologized to her, you would beg her not to call your parents. Invariably some disagreements led to fisticuffs, but we all made sure it didn't happen in front of the store. If any fights were about to occur, they had to take place down the street and around the corner.

Mr. Dave and Mrs. Emma's backyard also became a neighborhood playground. They had a basketball goal behind their house for their children but opened it to the neighborhood. They even provided a basketball for us to use. Buddy, Donald Ray, or Carl, their sons, monitored all of our games. Football and softball games took place on a vacant lot about one hundred yards down the street from the store.

Although our primary conversations were about girls and sports, we were not oblivious to the world around us. Racial segregation and discrimination permeated our everyday lives. Civil rights issues often came to our attention. Our parents told us that things were going to change. I was eight years old and in the fourth grade when, in 1954, the Supreme Court decided *Brown v. Board of Education of Topeka*. That decision gave our parents, our teachers, and Black folks in general high hopes that better days were ahead. We expected to soon be going to school with white kids. But "soon" never came for my classmates and me. The integration of schools in East Baton Rouge Parish didn't start until 1963, one year after I graduated from McKinley Senior High School.

And forty-seven years would pass after the *Davis, et al., v. East Baton Rouge School Board* lawsuit filed by my cousin Alex Pitcher and others, before the schools of Baton Rouge were declared desegregated by the U.S. District Court for the Middle District of Louisiana.

Looking back, I can honestly say that picking my cousin Alex Pitcher as my role model played a significant role in my journey toward the judiciary. Alex and my father were first cousins. Alex's father and my paternal grandfather were brothers. Alex was in the first graduating class from the Southern University Law School in 1952. He was one of the first Black attorneys to hang a shingle out in Baton Rouge. What first drew my attention to him was that he was a sharp dresser, and every visit he made to our house was a "happening." My dad would call his three brothers, Willie, George, and Emanuel, to come by our house and join him to hear Alex's commentary on the civil rights movement in and around the city, state, and nation. They would talk for hours as they sipped on their preferred adult beverage.

Alex was heavily involved in both the local and regional civil rights movement. He was the chief counsel for the National Association for the Advancement of Colored People (NAACP) in Baton Rouge, and in 1956 he filed the lawsuit to desegregate East Baton Rouge Parish schools. The suit, *Clifford Eugene Davis, Jr., et al. v. East Baton Rouge Parish School Board et al.*, was of interest to Black people all over the city. Joining Alex on the lawsuit pleading were local attorney Johnnie Jones; attorney A. P. Tureaud from New Orleans; and Thurgood Marshall, a highly acclaimed and publicized attorney for the NAACP and future U.S. Supreme Court justice. I would listen to their conversations. Alex would talk about the *Davis* case and how the lawyers planned to proceed in the court. I heard them talk about the U.S. Supreme Court and the *Brown* decision. Occasionally, neighbors would drop by to join in the conversation. Mr. Davis, the plaintiff in the *Davis, et al. v. East Baton Rouge School Board* case, lived in Valley Park. He would come by when he knew Alex was at our house. Though I was only ten or eleven years old at the time, I could tell that everyone admired Alex. I wanted to have that same admiration and respect when I grew up. I wanted to be like Alex.

Many of the boys with whom I shared time on the Owens Grocery bench ended up becoming carpenters, painters, brick masons, or craftsmen like their fathers, brothers, or uncles. Most of them turned out quite well. Only a few of us made it from the bench into college. A few also found their way to careers in the army. A few spent time in prison.

There were not many jobs for young Black boys at the time, and most of us worked as caddies at the Westdale Country Club Golf Course, currently named Webb Memorial Park Golf Course after a former mayor of the city. We'd jump a fence and cut through the wooded area separating Westdale, an all-white neighborhood, from Valley Park to get to the golf course. I always felt uneasy walking through the white neighborhood because of the racial attitudes and tension during that time.

Caddies had pay grades of A, B, or C, depending upon their age and experience. I was a C caddy and always ended up carrying the bag for the most inexperienced golfers. They always seemed to blame the caddy for their ineptness at the game. There were times when the N-word would be hurled around by a golfer at a missed easy shot, blaming it all on the caddy. The caddies put up with such abuse to make a few dollars.

I was about to move up to B caddy status when I was unceremoniously told to "get my ass off the golf course." I was sitting in the club locker room with Charles Tilley, another caddy, waiting out a very violent thunderstorm. The caddy shack, which was down the hill from the clubhouse, had a big hole in the roof and offered no protection for us during such a storm. The club pro didn't care. We were just niggers as far as he was concerned, and he often said so. As Tilley and I made our way across the golf course's parking lot, we unleashed a barrage of rocks at the pro and immediately took off running toward Valley Park. Tilley was not running toward home because he lived across town in Eden Park and ended up having to call his father to come to get him for fear of being arrested by the police. That incident ended my caddying career.

The loss of caddying opportunities didn't turn out to be so bad after all. A cousin, Eugene "Gene" Pitcher, referred me to the Southdowns Barber Shop. The barbers there needed someone to clean up the shop and shine shoes. Gene taught me how to polish and shine shoes well enough to keep the job, which turned out to be a far better gig than caddying. I hung on to this job all through the summer but let it go when football practice and school started.

## College Years

I entered Southern University as a college freshman for the summer session after graduating from McKinley in May 1962. The university was coming off of nearly two years of student unrest coinciding with sit-in demonstrations taking place all over the South. Southern students made their way to downtown Baton Rouge and sat at lunch counters at several different whites-only establishments. Many got arrested, sparking campus demonstrations and a protest march downtown. The trouble and unrest caused the university to be summarily closed by its president, Dr. Felton G. Clark. As high school students, we didn't participate in any of the college students' direct actions, though we wanted to. Our high school administrators encouraged us to stay on campus when there was even a hint that some might join the students marching from Southern to downtown. My parents cautioned me to stay out of campus demonstrations and reminded me that I was in school to get an education.

During that summer session, I did rather well, getting an A in math and history and a B in the freshman orientation class. When the fall semester started, I let my summer success lull me into a false sense of security. I got caught up in the excitement of football season and spent too much time admiring the beautiful young ladies on campus from all over the state. My friend, A. C. Stanberry, who was majoring in architecture, convinced me and his brother, Aaron, that we too should make architecture our college major. The freshman architecture curriculum was much different from that of liberal arts students. I felt cool walking around campus with my T-square and slide rule, but my grades took a nosedive due to my lack of discipline and my spending too much time in the student union. It took me two semesters to recognize that architecture was not what I was supposed to pursue. The lure of going to dances on campus and sporting events instead of finishing up projects due the next day was way too much for me, so I decided to change my major.

Once I did, I began looking at law school again. Like most students who want to become lawyers, I believed that political science was the major that would best prepare me for law school. My parents weren't thrilled with my choice. Their enthusiasm about me going to law school changed when the district attorney prosecuted my cousin Alex on a false "theft of client funds" charge. Alex was jailed, tried, convicted, and sentenced to a six-month jail term at Angola, the state's maximum-security prison. He was also disbarred; he could no longer practice law. The charges against him stemmed from his civil rights activities in and around Baton Rouge. The rumor circulating in our family was that District Attorney Sargent Pitcher, who was white and no relation, of course, found Alex to be a thorn in his side because of his civil rights leadership efforts. Some remarked that the DA needed to control "his N-Word cousin" because Alex was stirring up unrest in the Black community. Sargent Pitcher allegedly represented the White Citizens' Council, a devout segregationist group.

Years later, after I became an attorney, and while attending a Christmas party at attorney Walter Dumas's office, Family Court Judge Thomas Pugh asked me if I was related to Alex Pitcher. I told him Alex was my cousin. He wanted to know how Alex was doing, and I told him Alex was living in San Francisco and doing quite well. Judge Pugh told me he was an assistant district attorney and friendly with Alex when he practiced law in Baton Rouge. He told me that he was sorry for what happened to Alex and had tried to warn him that his civil rights activities could get him in trouble.

Alex ignored Judge Pugh's warnings and persisted in taking on the fight for civil rights in Baton Rouge. Most Black folks, especially our family, believed that the charges against Alex alleging theft of the client's funds were bogus and trumped up. Alex was tried before an all-white jury, found guilty, and ferried off to prison at Angola. The client from whom Alex allegedly misappropriated money was a distant cousin.

Alex's father, the Rev. Alex Pitcher Sr., and his brother, Rev. W. M. Pitcher, were financially well-off and wanted to make restitution. But the client was threatened and told that he could not accept money from Alex or his family. My cousin always contended that the funds in question were attorney's fees owed him for a series of transactions he had handled. Alex tendered the balance to the client's family after taking out his attorney's fees.

Alex moved his family to San Francisco and rebuilt his life. After I became an attorney, I offered to help him get his Louisiana bar license restored. He declined, saying he "wanted nothing from Louisiana." The thought of his treatment in Baton Rouge brought up so many bad memories that he didn't want to relive again. Alex's passion for civil rights did not end with the experience he had in Baton Rouge. He became the president of the San Francisco Bay Area NAACP, once in 1982 and again in 1994. He was employed by the City of San Francisco, heading up a housing program under Mayor Joseph Alioto's administration. In 1993, he was honored at a banquet held in his name that had a steering committee of more than fifty prominent citizens of San Francisco. Federal Judge Robert L. Carter, Southern District of New York, and former general counsel of the NAACP, was the guest speaker. When Alex died in January 2001, I attended his funeral and was amazed at how large the attendance was at his service. San Francisco's mayor, Willie Brown, and nearly the entire city council attended. Mayor Brown gave a short eulogy citing Alex's NAACP leadership and his strong advocacy for his community. The funeral procession drove through Hunters Point, an area Alex helped revitalize as the executive director of Bayview–Hunters Point Housing Development Corporation. People on the street corners stood at attention and saluted. Alex had indeed had a significant impact in his adopted home.

In 1994 Alex was again named president of the San Francisco chapter of the NAACP. During his five-year term, he promoted school integration, attempted to ease racial tensions with police, and rebuilt neighborhood programs and commerce. Community leaders hailed him as an unfailingly polite champion for the rights of people of all ethnicities, and in 1993 the community room at the City College of San Francisco

Southeast campus was renamed in his honor. Alex also received special awards for lifetime achievement from the NAACP's city chapter in both 1993 and 1999.

❧ ❧

Despite my parents' skepticism about what my life might be like if I pursued a legal career, I still liked the idea. Robert Frost's poem "The Road Not Taken," which my American literature class had analyzed, helped me make up my mind about choosing political science as my major, with law school as my ultimate goal. Although the road to becoming a lawyer was less traveled for Black men, it would be the road for me. My new major of political science was an excellent fit for me. My grades jumped to A's and B's in just about every course I took, except French. I particularly enjoyed the thought-provoking and challenging classes of Dr. Jewel Prestage, chairman of the Political Science Department; Professor Alex Willingham; and Dr. Henry Cobb, chairman of the History Department.

I got involved in student activities around campus and became an active member of the Pre-Law Society. Occasionally, the Pre-Law Society would host a Southern Law faculty member or law student who spoke to us about the law and law school. We got a chance to sit in on mock trials, an experience that fueled my desire to become a lawyer even more. I began hanging out at the law school as if I were already enrolled there.

At the close of my junior year, I applied to participate in a six-week summer work-study program in New Haven, Connecticut, sponsored by Yale University and Community Progress, Inc. (CPI), the city's antipoverty program. Community Progress and the Yale Department of Social Science had applied for and received a rather substantial grant from the federal government to encourage and train college students to take on jobs with antipoverty programs around the United States. I saw the program notice posted on the bulletin board in the Political Science Department, and having no set plans for the coming summer, I filled out an application on a whim.

Luckily, I was one of five students from Southern selected to participate in the Yale/CPI program in New Haven. We joined a group of approximately seventy students from colleges and universities all over the United States, twenty-five of whom were from Historically Black Colleges and Universities (HBCUs).

What was so exciting about this opportunity was that I would have a chance to spend the summer at Yale, an Ivy League university. Moreover, I would be paid a weekly stipend of $350 and given free room and board. Upon arrival, I was assigned to Stiles College as my summer residence, one of the university's newer on-campus dormitories.

The summer program focused on giving the participants a heavy dose of the country's socioeconomic and political problems as an orientation to the world of community action in the hope that we would consider jobs in President Lyndon Johnson's War on Poverty initiative. We talked a lot about how direct action and self-help could eliminate many of these problems with the proper community action focus. We were assigned to work at a government agency in New Haven and required to spend five days a week, four hours a day there. The rest of our time was devoted to classroom lectures and discussions. The lecturers were Yale faculty members or local political figures, including New Haven mayor Richard "Dick" Lee.

I was assigned to the New Haven City Planning Agency and worked on compiling land use surveys in targeted poverty-stricken neighborhoods as part of the city's urban renewal project. The program placed me in my first fully integrated work and academic environment. Having attended a segregated elementary school, graduated from a segregated high school, and now attending an HBCU, I was a bit apprehensive about my academic preparedness for this venture. I always had a strong sense of self-confidence when operating within the confines of my world, but the summer at Yale was unlike anything I had ever experienced.

Early on, there was a get-acquainted party on a beach on Long Island Sound. Our advisors told us we could bring our bathing suits to swim in the Sound if we wanted. We were a group of college students from all around the country who were just getting acquainted with one another. I decided to show off and swim to a large rock protruding out of the water. I saw several other swimmers out there and figured it would be an easy swim. It turned out that I misjudged the distance. I dove into the water and began swimming toward the rock. After swimming for a while, I flipped over on my back and began to float. I thought I was swimming in a straight direction, and I didn't realize that the waves were pushing me away from rather than toward my destination. Suddenly I heard screams and turned over to see that the guys on the rock were yelling at me. I was moving in the wrong direction and nearly panicked. I mustered up all the strength I had and swam until I reached the rock. When I made it, I was utterly exhausted. They could hardly pull me out of the water. I heard the lifeguard on his megaphone yelling for us to come back to shore. I felt I needed a boat to bring me back in. One of the guys on the rock offered to swim to a point where he could stand up and serve as my target. Another offered to swim beside me for direction.

I made it back to shore, exhausted and embarrassed by the commotion I had caused. But this experience taught me a valuable lesson in fortitude. I could have panicked and drowned in Long Island Sound, but I learned that one can overcome adversity even when things look dire if one has resolve. I made a bad decision—I knew it, and I learned from it.

Any uneasiness I felt in this integrated environment dissipated after the first week. I participated in classroom discussions and held my own with students from some of America's top schools. I began to realize that my McKinley High and Southern University training had prepared me much better than I first believed. My self-confidence grew stronger as the days and weeks passed. By the end of my summer at Yale, I was full of self-confidence and aware that I could successfully compete in any situation.

I became friends with two other members of the Yale program, Ronald Brown and Charles Johnson. During the regular school year Ronald attended Dartmouth, and Charles attended Yale. Lucia Faithful, another student in the program, invited the three of us to a summer outing at her house in Bedford, New York. Lucia picked Charles, Ron, and me up in her Volkswagen van one Saturday morning. Off we went to Bedford, which was about an hour's drive from New Haven. I didn't know it then but later learned that Bedford was one of the wealthiest communities in New York. The summer outing was to an annual party that Lucia gave. She invited her former high school classmates and other friends to hang out on the spacious grounds of her parents' estate. We, three Black young men, stood out among the thirty or so white guests there.

As the day of softball and volleyball drew to a close, we gathered to discuss pressing socioeconomic and political issues of the times. The Vietnam War figured most prominently as most of the males attending were eligible for the draft. It wasn't long before the conversation shifted to civil rights and the plight of Black people in America, and particularly those in the South.

Charles and Ron got a pass on most of the discussion because they attended Ivy League schools and were not from the South. Everyone assumed I would be the one to provide compelling personal stories of racial discrimination. I felt very uncomfortable doing so but did respond to a certain degree. I told everyone that I had felt the pain of discrimination, had been called "nigger" by white people for no apparent reason, and made to stand at the back of the bus as a kid growing up even though seats in the front were empty. I had been denied the right to eat at lunch counters, which had "Whites-only" signs. I told them the abuse and discrimination they read about and saw on television was real. No Black person was immune. I told them that Black southerners were hopeful that the passage of the 1964 Civil Rights Act would put an end to many of the indignities they had had to endure during years of racial segregation and discrimination.

Ron attended Harvard Law School and later told James Gray, another Harvard student from Baton Rouge, of our meeting at Yale in a summer program. James and I became friends when he returned to Baton Rouge, and we briefly practiced law together. He told me of his friendship with Ron and of Ron sharing that he met me in the Yale program. Unfortunately, I lost contact with Charles altogether.

I returned to Southern for the fall semester, feeling more confident than ever that I could make a difference in the world. My experience at Yale convinced me that I had what it took to compete on any level, anywhere, given the opportunity to do so.

## Coming of Age and the World of Work

I graduated from Southern University with a bachelor's degree in political science in August 1966. I was headed off to Sacramento, California, to take a job with the U.S. Department of Interior's Reclamation Bureau as a Job Corps program counselor. However, I kept delaying my start date with Job Corps. The agency even offered to pay for my travel if that was the cause of the delay. I really wanted a job closer to home. I was dating Harriet and intended to go to law school. I scanned the help-wanted ads of the *State-Times* newspaper, which came out in the afternoon. A job opening at Community Advancement, Inc. (CAI) caught my attention. The next day I dressed in a coat and tie and immediately made my way over to the agency's personnel office.

CAI was a federal community action program created to provide a broad range of services to the poor and underprivileged in Baton Rouge. It grew out of President Lyndon Johnson's 1964 Great Society, which included a broad range of policy initiatives, with the chief goal of ending poverty. Through the Federal Office of Economic Opportunity, programs were developed to be replicated around the country that would address a community's basic needs and help it alleviate poverty within. For Baton Rouge and other cities that meant teaching community leaders how to advocate for the needs and services of their community, including (1) providing job opportunities for the underserved population in their neighborhood, (2) providing early childhood education (Head Start) for preschool children, and (3) enlisting community leaders and volunteers to work in concert with the agency to fulfill its goals.

CAI intended to launch an employment office in the South Baton Rouge Neighborhood Service Center and was recruiting staffers. I filled out a job application and waited about an hour for an interview. John Cantrell, the operations director, met with me. He asked me about my knowledge of CAI, the War on Poverty, and my community involvement. I told him of my Valley Park roots and my volunteer record with the Neighborhood Service Center, as well as my experiences in Connecticut with both Community Progress, Inc., and the New Haven Planning Commission. He told me he would be making hiring decisions within the week, and I would hear back from him.

CAI ran several Head Start programs and had nine Neighborhood Service Centers scattered throughout East Baton Rouge Parish. One of the Neighborhood Service Centers was in Valley Park, my old neighborhood. Its initial office was located at the New Gideon Baptist Church, diagonally across the street from my house. After the center opened, I would visit to see if there was anything I could do to help out. When I wasn't attending class at Southern, I often distributed flyers around the area that advised residents about upcoming community meetings and events.

Community activism, the core value of the center's efforts, was directed through the community leaders' advisory committee, which had a director and several paid neighborhood workers (community organizers), whose job was to help the residents achieve the center's goals and objectives.

Neighborhoods like Valley Park had many problems that had been neglected by local city government. There were drainage issues, open ditches and exposed sewerage, inadequate recreational facilities, poor educational and employment opportunities to organize the people around. Community leaders cited various inequities at community meetings and invited the news media to spread their dissatisfactions in the hope of pressuring government officials to respond. Residents were encouraged to attend city council meetings and voice their anguish about the lack of attention given to Baton Rouge's Black population.

At one point, Mr. Elroy Wells, the owner of Wells' Place Lounge, a neighborhood bar, was shot to death. The police chose not to arrest his assailant, who claimed that he had acted in self-defense. I grabbed the microphone at a neighborhood protest rally and vehemently labeled the lack of police action as a travesty of justice.

How could it have been self-defense? I questioned. The shooter left the bar, went to the trunk of his car, retrieved a rifle, turned around, and fired several shots into the building, one of which struck Mr. Wells, killing him instantly. Shortly before his murder, Mr. Wells had evicted the assailant. In retaliation for that perceived insult to his manhood, the assailant randomly fired his rifle into the building. The shooter, whose street name was "Tiny Tim," was reputed to be a paid police informant. It appeared that the connection gave him a "license to kill" in Baton Rouge, for he was neither arrested nor indicted for the murder of Elroy Wells. Years later, when I became an assistant district attorney, I found Tiny Tim sitting in the DA's office chatting with several detectives, apparently still on the payroll.

After my interview, I received a call from CAI's personnel office informing me that I had been hired and assigned to the South Baton Rouge Employment Agency. My start date was a week away. I asked for written confirmation before I notified Job Corps that I would not be coming to California after all.

My first paid position as a college graduate was that of a job developer with CAI's South Baton Rouge Employment office. There was negligible orientation and training for my position. I was told to reach out to employers throughout the parish and solicit jobs our program constituents could fill. I dutifully set up appointments to meet with various business owners and managers, only to be told when I arrived that the executives were busy or out of the office. Considering the racial situation in Baton Rouge in 1966, my task proved to be a daunting one.

We would often receive job descriptions from employers who knew we couldn't fill them. On one occasion an employer asked me to help his company find an African American to fill a cost accountant position. When I contacted the lone Black CPA in New Orleans, he said: "We are few and far between. If you find one, send him to me first." I did have some success in getting several people hired as short-term day or week laborers, and I was able to place a few of our applicants in secretarial positions. It became apparent that there was a need for a simple training program that could prepare community members for gainful employment in skilled jobs.

I had to come to grips with numerous canceled appointments. These cancellations often happened only after I showed up, and the person I was to meet discovered I was Black. The level of racism I faced daily was dispiriting. On occasion I would meet with a personnel director and be told his company had no job openings, even though it was running newspaper job ads. The constant negative responses from employers began to take a toll on my confidence. I was starting to wonder if I had made a mistake turning down the Job Corps opportunity in California. Fortunately, a new initiative, the In-School Neighborhood Youth Corps (NYC), rescued me from the employment agency. Claire Schexnayder, a very nice and well-connected white woman, was named director, and I was named the assistant director. My work experience changed dramatically.

The In-School NYC program provided paid training, work experience, and supportive services needed by low-income youth. The program encouraged them to stay in school, develop their occupational potential, and obtain regular competitive employment. Continued school enrollment was encouraged. Participants were also authorized to work an average of ten hours a week during the approximately thirty-eight-week program year. The minimum wage for enrollees was $1.25 an hour.

I was still in the job development business but was now working toward getting high school students prepared for and acclimated to the world of work. Students would sign up through their school counselor's office. I would canvass employers for jobs that students working part-time could fulfill and match teens with employers' job openings. When making cold calls to employers, the reception was far more welcoming when they knew I represented a youth program. The In-School NYC program received its initial funding from a grant of $171,700 from the U.S. Department of Labor.

I started working there on January 3, 1967, even though I had applied for admission to pursue a master's degree from the LSU School of Government a few months earlier. My grad school application was accepted along with a graduate school assistantship. My goal was to pursue a master's degree while working simultaneously at Community Advancement.

I thought grad school would help me get a draft deferment, but Uncle Sam had other thoughts. My draft notice arrived. The Draft Board denied my application for a military deferment to attend graduate school. I was headed off to the U.S. Army. Little did I know then that my letter of acceptance to graduate school would prove valuable later on.

### Off to the Army

I started basic training at Fort Polk, which is right outside of Leesville, Louisiana. In the five months since I graduated college, I had gained fifteen pounds and now weighed close to two hundred pounds. I was a twenty-one-year-old bachelor with a college degree driving a relatively new burgundy Chevrolet Impala with bucket seats and a stick on the floor. I had a decent job and money in my pocket, and I partied plenty.

Before I knew it, I had gained a lot of extra weight. Thanks to the army's rigorous basic training, it didn't take long for me to lose all the weight I had gained.

I excelled in all areas of basic training save one: accuracy on the firing range. I barely qualified as a marksman, but it kept me from having to repeat basic training. From this experience I quickly learned that I needed a prescription change for my eyeglasses.

After my first month of basic training, I got a weekend pass to travel off of the post. Harriet, my college girlfriend, who would soon become my fiancée and then my wife, came to pick me up and drove me back to Baton Rouge. We had a great weekend, visiting family and friends. One of her friends rode back to Fort Polk with us so that Harriet would not have to drive home alone. Two weeks later, I got another weekend pass and caught a ride with two fellas heading to Zachary, Louisiana, a few miles north of Baton Rouge. With the end of basic training getting near and the specter of going to Vietnam ever-present, I was anxious to spend as much time with Harriet as I could.

When it was time to return to Fort Polk, I called the two soldiers with whom I had driven home. They told me that they had decided to take a couple more days off before going back to Fort Polk. I had a real dilemma. I couldn't drive my car. My father wasn't well and not in a position to drive me back to Fort Polk. Harriet had a commitment that prevented her from doing likewise. There were no Trailways or Greyhound buses headed in that direction until the following day. By chance, I called the Baton Rouge airport and found seats available on a flight to Lake Charles scheduled to depart around 5:00 p.m. Lake Charles was only about one hour south of Fort Polk, and I assumed I could catch a bus from there and make it to Fort Polk before reveille. My mom and dad scraped up enough cash to cover my airfare. This flight would be my very first plane ride. The plane was propeller driven, and the ride was bumpy all the way and quite scary. I made it to Lake Charles, and my plan seemed to be working until I got to the Greyhound bus station. It turned out there were no buses to Fort Polk until the next morning. I slept in the bus station overnight, caught the first bus out in the morning, made it to the post, and walked up just as everyone was standing in formation for callout. That episode got me an Article 15 under the Uniform Code of Military Justice, which gives a commanding officer the authority to mete out punishment for minor offenses, such as being absent without leave. My punishment was a week of extra duty cleaning up the company headquarters, as well as a dressing down by the company commanding officer (CO), an African American army captain. He took me aside and said that I should be setting a better example as the only Black college graduate in the entire company, but I was doing just the opposite. I was absolutely embarrassed and assured him that this would not happen again.

I completed basic training at Fort Polk and received orders to report to Fort Gordon, Georgia. I was given the Military Occupational Specialty (MOS) of personnel specialist and assigned to a job at Transfer Point, where soldiers leaving the service were discharged. My job was to screen a soldier's Military Personnel File (201) to ensure all required documents were complete.

About four months into my duty at Fort Gordon, I was temporarily assigned to the Third Army POR (Process for Overseas Replacement) team. The team was responsible for processing large troop movements overseas, primarily to Vietnam. I traveled to Fort Campbell, Kentucky, to help the team deploy the Second Brigade of the 101st Airborne. Upon arriving, we went to work immediately. I was assigned to the 201-file check, ensuring that next-of-kin information, insurance information, shot records, etc., were in order. After soldiers left my station, they boarded buses and were off to the airport and Vietnam. The team processed nearly four thousand troops, working day and night for a solid week before getting a breather.

As we were wrapping up, our team was called together by the colonel in charge. He told us that we were being assigned to the 101st because nearly half of the troops in personnel with the 101st had too little time left in the army to complete a full tour of duty in Vietnam. The colonel asked if any of us had a reason why we could not accept this assignment. Several soldiers raised their hands, as did I. One said, "Sir, we are not Airborne." He said, "Don't worry, we'll take care of that after we get in-country." I said: "Sir, I am scheduled to get married next month. We sent out invitations and have already spent a lot of money on the wedding." With that, he agreed to not include me in the Vietnam deployment with the 101st.

Harriet and I got married on December 24, 1967. Now I had to think about supporting a wife when I got out of the army. I received orders for a duty station transfer to Baumholder, Germany, which turned out to be the coldest place this Louisiana boy had ever been in. After I'd spent a couple of months overseas, Harriet and I decided that she should take a sabbatical leave from her job as a speech therapist with the East Feliciana Parish School Board and join me in Germany. She came over at the end of her spring 1968 semester.

My first sergeant was adamantly opposed to me bringing my wife to Germany and tried to get the company commander to rescind the approval he had given me to live off post. I had gotten negative vibes from the first sergeant from the day I arrived and began working in the Orderly Room as a clerk. I believe it was a "color thing" with him, and he didn't try to hide it.

I rented a small apartment in downtown Baumholder from a wonderful German family whose last name was Hikke. The Hikkes included Harriet and me in many of their social gatherings and invited us to join them when they attended weekend beer festivals.

My most daunting experience while stationed in Germany began on August 20, 1968, when the Russians invaded Czechoslovakia. A red alert, which meant emergency, was issued. Red alerts required soldiers to immediately report to their duty stations. It was midnight. I jumped up, got dressed, went outside, and tried starting my Renault Dauphine to no avail. I went back into my apartment and tried calling the company, but my calls were unable to get through. It was too far to walk in the dark of the night, so I lay back across the bed and told Harriet that I would wait until daylight to hitch a ride in.

When daylight hit, I caught a ride on the back of a large tractor-trailer truck and made it onto the post. When I arrived, I saw that everyone had a weapon. My platoon leader, a noncommissioned officer, told me that the first sergeant was furious that I was late and considered me absent without leave (AWOL). I tried to explain, but the first sergeant didn't want to hear excuses and kept saying that I didn't come in at the alert's first notice. After receiving a tongue lashing, I drew my weapon from the arms room and assembled with my platoon. By the end of the day, the emergency abated, and things started to calm down. But the first sergeant was determined to make me move back on the post and asked the CO to give me an Article 15 for an alleged "absent without leave" infraction. Fortunately, we had a West Point graduate as CO, and he was pretty reasonable. He knew me when I worked in the Orderly Room as a clerk and from my Command Information class participation. I explained to him what happened, hoping to mitigate my punishment. He told me he had to live with the first sergeant, so he would go along with giving me an Article 15 and fourteen days of extra duty. However, since I was a specialist 4th class, and the highest-ranking soldier assigned extra duty, he directed me to supervise the other soldiers pulling duty with me. The CO also told me he would not make me move back on the post, which was a great relief.

While I was upstairs in a Command Information class, after my first week of extra duty, the CO called me to the front of the class and told me that I had passed the test for promotion to sergeant E5. He congratulated me and then pinned a set of E5 stripes on my shoulders. I had taken the test weeks earlier but didn't expect to hear anything for a few weeks. The CO also told me to forget about completing the extra duty that had been assigned to me.

I went downstairs, and as I was passing by the Orderly Room, the first sergeant said, "Congratulations, Sergeant Pitcher, on your promotion—and forget about that extra duty." I told him the CO had mentioned that upstairs.

Because the draft superseded my graduate school attendance, LSU informed me that the assistantship they had offered me would still be available when I got out of the army. In early September 1968 I filed a DD 1049 Personnel Action Form with the Department of the Army requesting an early discharge to attend graduate school. Thanks to Charles Jones, a friend from my Southern undergrad years who was working at Eighth Army Headquarters in Bad Kreuznach, Germany, my 1049 went through without a hitch. I received orders for an early discharge, which would put me home in time for the spring semester in January 1969.

Before returning to the United States, Harriet and I celebrated our first wedding anniversary in Paris. We spent three days of a five-day bus excursion there over the 1968 Christmas holidays. The trip was quite memorable. We visited the Eiffel Tower, the Louvre, the Arc de Triomphe, and Versailles, as well as other notable Parisian sites.

After our Paris trip, I had to make a quick turnaround to get Harriet to the airport in Frankfurt, Germany, for her return trip to the United States. It was great to be getting out of the army early and heading off to graduate school. Harriet thought my graduate school decision was questionable, in that all I had talked about for the last year was law school. She wanted to know if I had given up on that dream. I assured her that I had not.

The Soldiers and Sailors Civil Relief Act guaranteed draftees that they could get their jobs back with former employers upon returning from the army. When I reported to CAI to reclaim my old job, I found it was not available. I could, however, become the administrative assistant to the director of the Manpower Training Program, which was comparable in pay to my old position. Rev. Ed Popleon was the director of the Manpower Program, and Lee Wesley, a good friend, was the assistant director. The job had flexible hours and afforded me time to work on a master's degree at LSU. I signed up for a nine-hour course load but soon found out that it was too much to handle while working full-time, so I dropped one of my courses.

As the administrative assistant, my job was to develop employment opportunities for the unemployed and the underemployed from underserved and low-income communities. The remedial education component of the Manpower Program proved to be the most successful of all. It took high school graduates and tutored them in subjects covered on qualifying exams for operator positions at chemical plants in and around the Baton Rouge area.

I decided not to attend graduate school during the summer and instead applied for the new summer prelaw program at the Southern University Law School. Now I could begin to focus on my true long-term employment goal—becoming an attorney.

The Council on Legal Education Opportunity, Inc. (CLEO) sponsored the summer program. As a nonprofit program, CLEO's goal was to expand minority and low-income students' opportunities to attend law school. The program was modeled after an eight-week prelaw program put on at Harvard in 1965. Students in the Harvard program were undergrads exposed to select topics from a first-year law school curriculum. Having this experience would assist students in gaining admission to law school and better ensure their success. The Southern Law School CLEO program ran for six weeks and included individuals who had already received undergraduate degrees. If a participant passed, law school admission was almost assured, along with scholarship funds to help defray the cost of tuition and books. This prelaw program was exactly what I needed. The classes were in the morning, and Mr. Popleon permitted me to make up my time by working evenings and weekends.

I was juggling a job and the summer prelaw program when we learned that Harriet was pregnant. The big question now was whether I could afford to go to law school. We had already experienced one miscarriage. Having Harriet running back and forth to work during this pregnancy might precipitate another. We decided to put law school off one more year and concentrate on assuring a successful outcome to her pregnancy. Our beautiful baby girl was born on January 23, 1969, and we named her Kyla Dean.

Several months into my job with the Manpower Program, W. W. Williams, director of the Neighborhood Service Center Systems for CAI, told me he was looking for an assistant director and suggested that I apply. I took this as "a wink and a nod" that the position would be mine if I wanted it. I did apply, and shortly after that, I became assistant director of the Neighborhood Service Center Systems for Community Advancement, Inc.

The Neighborhood Service Center endeavored to help low-income families overcome their hardships and exit poverty. There were nine such centers in East Baton Rouge, headed by a director and staffed with a secretary and several neighborhood workers. The neighborhood workers' job was to canvass their assigned territories, assess the residents' eligibility for services provided by the parish or state agencies, and channel them to the appropriate social service agencies based on need. Each of the centers had to develop a set of goals. As the assistant director, it was my job to help the centers to achieve them. The job had me attending numerous community meetings all over East Baton Rouge Parish.

When I took the position, I did not know that the centers' directors were almost uniformly up in arms against Mr. Williams, which unexpectedly thrust me into the middle of operational turmoil. I knew most of the directors before coming aboard and had reasonably good relations with them. Suddenly I found myself mediating conflicts between people who were not only much older than I was but also quite obstinate, especially when getting together as a group. Although I had no formal management training, I quickly had to figure out the best way to "unruffle their feathers" when arguments flared at staff meetings.

My first de-escalation tactic was to spend time with each director one-on-one and help them brainstorm resolutions to both community and administrative issues. Mr. Williams started letting me run the meetings, which enabled him to sidestep caustic relations with the centers' directors. Their complaints ranged from lack of support from Mr. Williams for various program initiatives to needing more staff and better pay. Providing the individual center directors with a chance to vent generally calmed things down. After about six months on the job, Mr. Williams came by my office and informed me he had resigned and recommended that I assume his position. He told me he had accepted a position at Southern University as the director of their Alcohol and Drug Addiction Program.

I became the Neighborhood Service Center Systems acting director and applied for the permanent position when it was advertised. Several of the individual center directors also applied. With this competition for the Systems directorship at hand, our once cordial staff meetings again became raucous. Some of my competitors made end runs with CAI board members, disparaging their fellow directors in the process. Charlie Granger, director of the South Baton Rouge Neighborhood Service Center, got the position. I was disappointed. I thought my interview had gone well. I knew the program in and out and all of the budgeting issues that needed fixing. My mistake was that I didn't lobby CAI board members. Charlie was more politically savvy than I was at the time, which gave him the upper hand. My only solace was that I did get a nice raise after losing out on the job when Charlie Tapp, CAI's executive director, realized that I would have to carry a lot of the administrative load and flipped the job descriptions of the director and assistant director, giving the field duties to Charlie Granger. Losing the Systems directorship reignited my desire to attend law school. That loss turned out to be a blessing in disguise. Like Mr. Williams, I began to plot my exit strategy.

### Off to Law School

I finally resigned from my job at Community Advancement and headed off to Southern University School of Law for the 1970 fall semester. During the first couple of months I also worked at an employment agency I helped start. The agency was thriving, but working there negatively impacted my law school study time. I learned the meaning of the adage "law school is a jealous mistress." It was nearly impossible to meet the demands of law school and hold down a job. I studied ten to twelve hours a day over the entire Christmas holidays so that my law school career would not end prematurely. That concentrated study helped me survive my first semester and reinforced my law school studies for the semesters ahead. During the second semester, I was elected president of the Student Bar Association for the 1971–72 school year by just one vote. My opponent was so confident he would win reelection that he went off drinking to celebrate with a classmate, and neither of them remembered to vote!

As the semester drew to a close, we also learned that Dean Vanue B. Lacour was stepping down as the head of the Law School. He had taken the helm only for one year after A. A. Lenoir, the founding dean of Southern's Law School, retired and took a faculty position at Howard University Law School. We learned pretty quickly that attorney Jesse N. Stone of Shreveport, Louisiana, would be our new dean. This was welcome news to many of us because through one of our classmates, S. P. Davis, Stone had a sterling reputation as a civil rights lawyer and leader in the Shreveport and north Louisiana area. We were sure that having someone like Attorney Stone leading us would help prepare us for the civil rights battles we all anticipated fighting once we entered the practice of law. I came to learn that he was also a classmate of my cousin Alex Pitcher in the first graduating class from the Southern University Law School. They both fully embraced former dean Lenoir's challenge to take up the mantle to fight for civil rights and justice, which was a constant refrain, according to his students. My cousin Alex focused his efforts in Baton Rouge, whereas Jesse Stone concentrated on Shreveport and north Louisiana.

Southern didn't offer a summer session when I was enrolled there, so I enrolled in an evidence course taught by Prof. George Pugh at LSU Law School. There was one other Black student in the class, who I later learned was Ralph Tyson. It turned out that I was the sole visiting Black student, and Ralph was the sole resident Black student. That summer, we made up LSU Law School's total diverse population of two. Some assumed that I would be transferring to LSU in the fall. As the newly elected president of the Student Bar Association (SBA) at Southern, I felt compelled to fulfill my responsibilities there. I also thought that it would have been inappropriate to ditch Southern for LSU. Ralph and I began a friendship that would inextricably tie us together for the rest of our lives, though we did not know it at the time.

After summer school, several members of my Student Bar leadership team and I were invited, all expenses paid, to attend the National Bar Association (NBA) annual meeting in Atlanta, Georgia. The NBA meeting turned out to be one of the highlights of my Student Bar tenure. I was in awe of the high caliber of the Black attorneys, stalwarts of the civil rights movement, and renowned political leaders from all over the country who attended. I was amazed by their willingness to meet with law students to discuss their successes and the law profession. I made a list of individuals I wanted to invite to participate in Southern's Law Week activities in the upcoming year. I had to let potential speakers know we didn't have travel or honorarium funds. Everyone I approached encouraged me to invite them, and they would see what they could work out.

Returning from Atlanta, I was excited to start spearheading Student

Bar activities and immerse myself in my academic pursuits. Law Week planning began immediately, although it didn't occur until the spring semester. By starting early, I was determined to make this the best Law Week ever.

After the Christmas holidays, we were back in school taking final exams when, on January 10, 1972, someone came into our classroom and told us that "holy hell" had broken out in downtown Baton Rouge. A shootout had taken place between the police and a group of Black Muslims. The law school administrators instructed us to stay clear of that area because a riot was in progress.

Later that day, I learned from radio and television news accounts that shooting broke out between the police and eighteen Black Muslims who had blocked a portion of North Boulevard near the old Temple Theatre. Allegedly, one of the Muslims pulled a pistol from his jacket, and a hail of bullets erupted between the police and the Muslims within a few minutes, leaving two of the Muslims and four police officers dead. The reports also indicated that in addition to the dead, thirty-one others were wounded.

After the confrontation, Mayor Woody Dumas put a curfew in place from 5:30 p.m. to 6:00 a.m. and requested the assistance of the National Guard from Governor John McKeithen. The governor responded with a callout of seven hundred National Guardsmen to back up the police, sheriff's deputies, and state police to help quell any further outbreaks of violence. Eddie Bauer, chief of police for the City of Baton Rouge, was quoted in the *State-Times* newspaper the following day as saying, "Authorities believe sympathizers with the group that triggered yesterday's shootout may attempt to come to Baton Rouge from other states." The *State-Times* also quoted Stanley Berthelot, the Louisiana state police commander, as saying he had urged agencies elsewhere in the state to take precautions for "armed and dangerous militants, possibly en route from other states."

News reports indicated that the group was made up of persons from California and Illinois who had gathered in Baton Rouge sometime around New Year. According to many, it was a mystery why they wanted to provoke a confrontation with the police, which started when they purposely blocked off North Boulevard with a line of their vehicles. When the police arrived to clear the street for traffic, the group of Muslims lined up in the street, shoulder to shoulder, arms crossed, and faced the approaching line of police officers when the shooting erupted.

## The Rumor Center

After this incident, the city was placed on lockdown and a curfew imposed. Two days after the shootout I got a call from Joyce Magee, secretary to Charlie Tapp, executive director of Community Advancement, Inc. (CAI), about a meeting he wanted me to attend. Charlie requested that I come over to CAI right away to meet with him and a couple of attorneys from the U.S. Department of Justice (DOJ) to talk about the North Boulevard incident. I was somewhat surprised and dumbfounded as to why someone from the Justice Department wanted to meet with me about the shooting incident since I was nowhere near North Boulevard that day. Upon arriving, I learned that George Bayhi, an LSU law student, was also invited to the meeting. George had worked at CAI as a counselor in the In-School NYC program. The two attorneys from DOJ explained that they were with the Community Service branch of the Justice Department, and it was their job to help communities work through incidents such as the one that had just occurred on North Boulevard. One of the techniques they employed with great success involved establishing a Rumor Center that citizens could call to fact-check rumors that were beginning to spread through the community. One such rumor that had everyone on edge alleged that caravans of Black Muslims were headed to Baton Rouge from California and Illinois. No one seemed to know where the rumor started, but it spread through Baton Rouge like wildfire.

Charlie said Community Advancement would pay George and me to run the Rumor Center. We were to hire law students from our respective law schools to assist us. As codirectors, we would each be paid ten dollars per hour, and our law student assistants would earn eight dollars per hour. Initially, they wanted the Rumor Center to take calls from 1:00 p.m. to midnight. However, calls generally stopped coming in around 9:00 p.m., so we started shutting down at 10:00 p.m. The Rumor Center's phone numbers were announced via public service announcements (PSAs) over radio and television. The PSAs encouraged people to call in if they wanted to check the veracity of rumors they heard.

The law students had a script to follow when responding to inquiries from the public. We wrote down the callers' questions or concerns for the attorneys from the Justice Department to review. Our job was to debunk rumors.

The top floor of a building on North Street housed the call center. George and I were the only ones with keys to the building, which meant that one of us had to be present at all times to open up and allow the students whom we had employed to gain access. The location and the names of the persons fielding the calls were kept private for security purposes.

The first couple of days the Rumor Center was open, calls flooded in with all sorts of outlandish stories. Because the North Boulevard incident involved Black Muslims and the police, racist insults were frequent. Our Justice Department supervisor warned us that we would receive these kinds of calls and told us to ignore the vitriol and try to help defuse the already tense situation in the city.

Calls began to dissipate after a week and became almost nonexistent after two weeks. We closed the Rumor Center and turned all of our call logs over to the Justice Department. I often wished I had kept copies of the call logs for a postmortem on that attempt to quiet a city in turmoil. One of the things I learned was that Baton Rouge's racial divide was more pronounced than I had ever imagined. The calls to the Rumor Center revealed layers of deep-seated racial attitudes lying below the city's veneer. Hopefully, our efforts helped tamp down the tension a bit.

I refocused on my law school studies and Student Bar business. During the first semester I invited several judges and lawyers I had met at the National Bar Association annual meeting to participate in our Law Week activities. My outreach paid dividends. Justice Lloyd O. Brown of the Ohio Supreme Court; the Hon. Frankie Freeman, chairman of the U.S. Civil Rights Commission; and George Haley, chief counsel of the U.S. Urban Mass Transportation Administration, U.S. Department of Transportation, all accepted my invitation and agreed to cover their own expenses.

Dean Stone and several local attorneys sponsored a lavish reception for our invited guests. Since I had only seven hundred dollars to run Student Bar programs for the entire year, I turned to Charles Jones, president of Southern's Student Government Association (SGA), for financial assistance. My pitch to him was that this would be an excellent opportunity to expose both law students and undergrads to nationally renowned speakers involved in the law, politics, and civil rights. Charles agreed to join in. With the benefit of undergraduates' student funds, we invited Judge George Crockett of Detroit, Michigan, to be our luncheon speaker. Judge Crockett was later elected to the U.S. House of Representatives, representing Michigan's Thirteenth Congressional District. Charles was later elected to both the Louisiana House of Representatives and Senate.

The Law Week program, as I had hoped, was an overwhelming success. Not only did the law students benefit from the inspirational presentations by our invited guests, but the Southern University community, students and faculty, from all parts of the campus packed the seminar rooms each day of the program.

The SBA was also responsible for the Patterson Moot Court Competition. Traditionally third-year students served as judges, and second-year appellate advocacy students presented oral arguments. I proposed to Dean Stone that we invite Eighteenth and Nineteenth Judicial District Court judges to serve as appellate judges for our moot court competition. Judge Luther Cole and Judge Eugene McGehee of the Nineteenth Judicial District Court, and Judge Edward Engolio of the Eighteenth Judicial District Court, served as the three-judge panel for our competition. Clyde Tidwell, our appellate advocacy professor, selected the problem for the competition, paired up the teams, and set briefing schedules.

As I recall, the issues dealt with an alleged illegal arrest under the stop-and-frisk police procedure in effect at the time. I represented the appellant. The law was not on my client's side. I prepared my brief, as did my classmates, and we delivered them to the judges. I argued vigorously during oral argument for reversal based upon the lack of probable cause to stop my client. The judges handed down their ruling, followed by a critique of the student lawyers' briefs and oral presentation.

The judges commented that the law was not on my side in my case and denied my client's appeal. But they unanimously agreed that I was the most outstanding advocate that night. They also gave high marks to S. P. Davis and Barry Edwards. The three of us ended up sharing the Patterson Moot Court Outstanding Advocate's Award for the 1971–72 academic year.

In an open letter to East Baton Rouge's voters years later, Judge Eugene McGehee, now retired, joined Judge Lewis Doherty in endorsing my candidacy for a seat on the Nineteenth Judicial District Court. After I won that election, Judge Cole, now Justice Cole of the Louisiana Supreme Court, swore me in at my investiture. He told everyone that "he first met me when I was a student at Southern University Law School, and he knew then that my knowledge of the law would take me as far as I wanted to go."

Both before and during my law school enrollment, there were always questions about Southern University Law School's viability and whether to relocate it to north Louisiana. The law school was historically under-funded and was hanging on primarily because of its underpaid but ded-icated faculty and staff. Every student feels their law degree has worth and value. When that law degree is disparaged, it has a chilling effect upon graduates and their ability to market themselves to potential cli-ents. Such was the situation when Hilry Huckaby, a Southern Law alum, filed a million-dollar lawsuit against the State of Louisiana and Southern University Law School, claiming that the law school education was inad-equate. He maintained that he failed the bar exam three times because he was inadequately prepared, alleging that his law curriculum was unequal to those offered at other state-supported institutions. Along with mem-bers of the law school student body, I was incensed by this lawsuit. We felt that the suit adversely affected and devalued our law degrees and provided ammunition to those who opposed the law school's existence and continually clamored to shut it down or move it to north Louisiana. Although we knew that much of what Huckaby was complaining about had merit, we questioned whether his lawsuit was the way for our law school to gain parity. After meeting with the Student Bar members and speaking to several faculty members, I felt that, as Student Bar president,

I needed to make a statement regarding the Southern University Law School's merits. I drafted a letter in response to Huckaby's lawsuit and sent it to the *State-Times*. On October 8, 1971, the newspaper published my statement under the title "Student Bar Group Answers Criticism of SU Law School" as follows:

> The Southern University Student Bar Association today issued a statement defending the Southern University Law School, branded as an inadequate institution in a $1 million lawsuit filed here this week. A former Southern law student filed the suit here Monday in state district court. The suit noted that the former student failed the state bar examination three times and charged that the school's law courses were faulty, inadequate and unequal to those offered at other state-supported institutions. Fred Pitcher, president of the student group, released the following statement: "The Student Bar Association of Southern University Law School feels that the future of black legal education and black attorneys in Louisiana has been viciously questioned by recent developments. Southern University Law School, the only predominantly black institution of legal training in Louisiana, has for many years been the training center for the development of black attorneys in the state and other states in the U.S. The role of Southern University Law School has been, and continues to be, that of bridging the gap between the legal needs of the black community and the amount of adequate legal assistance by black attorneys. The record reveals that the black enrollment in the white-oriented law schools of this state has been few. Those graduated therefrom have been fewer. If not Southern University the tasks of training legal minds under conditions of second-rate facilities and insufficient funds from the State Legislature and Board of Education, but to say that we are fully satisfied with the school's past laurels or the total academic milieu would be erroneous. Southern University Law School is experiencing a period of expansion. This year we have the largest enrollment in history 101, comprised of students

[from] throughout the country, both black and white. Many of them are gifted and promising students who are dedicated to the idea that equal justice in America will prevail. Thus, the increased enrollment of the school, the unique legal needs of the black community, and the ever-changing developments in legal education demand increased facilities and appropriations. From our perspective, this will require a concerted effort of the state government, the University, the faculty, alumni, and the black community. However, all the parties concerned must have the basic belief that, as Professor Harry Edwards of University of Michigan Law School has said, 'if "equal justice under law" is to be the basic rule of the judicial game in America, then there must be more black players on the team.' Southern University Law School has and must continue to meet the challenge with renewed vigor."

After my letter was published, I received an overwhelming show of support from my law school colleagues, the Southern University academic community, and the Black community for defending the law school against this assault.

As I ended my junior year, the law school experienced another change in leadership. This time, Dean Stone was stepping down to take a position as an assistant secretary of education, which caught us all by surprise. Since I was president of the Student Bar, his door was always open to me, and I didn't have to have an appointment to see him. Throughout the school year, I often met with him on SBA business. During our meetings, he sometimes shared his thoughts and ideas about the practice of law, politics, and life in general. After learning of his intent to depart, I went in to chat with him as I was concerned about the law school's viability with him leaving after only one year. He revealed to me that his long-term game plan was to return to Southern, not as dean but as president. The Louisiana State Department of Education position was only a head fake to get his politics lined up and some higher education administrative experience behind him. This was mind-blowing to me, but it revealed how strategic he was. My encounters with Dean Stone while I served as president of the Student Bar were akin to a class in Politics 101. True to his prediction, Jesse Nealand Stone became President Stone of the Southern University system in 1974.

In 1972, at the beginning of my last year of law school, Dr. Leon Netterville, the president of Southern University, appointed attorney Louis Berry, another civil rights stalwart, as Stone's successor. Given Attorney Berry's credentials, Dr. Netterville, I am sure, hoped he could lend some stability to the law school following the frequent changing of its leadership. He was a terrific teacher, an outstanding lawyer, and had been an adjunct member of the faculty for a couple of years. The law school needed an administrator to advocate on its behalf to the university's central administration and the legislature for more funding and student aid. It was obvious that the law school was not high on the list of priorities for the university's administration, which I am sure was frustrating for Dean Berry and probably led to his departure after only two years on the job.

Although I was no longer the SBA president, I was still intricately involved in law school politics and deeply concerned about the law school's existence, not only for me but for those who would come later.

With Dean Berry's resignation, Jesse Stone, the newly appointed president of Southern University, now faced the same task as Dr. Netterville—to appoint a law school dean who could bring some stability to the school. He turned to Professor B. K. Agnihotri, who had been on the faculty since 1968 and was appointed associate dean in 1978. Although Agnihotri's appointment was initially not well received by law school alumni and members of the Black bar, his devotion and dedication to improving the law school were quite apparent, winning over the naysayers to his appointment. He brought a unique administrative skill set to the law school that helped to stave off funding, political, and accreditation challenges throughout a twenty-seven-year tenure as dean and chancellor.

As I began the fall semester of my senior year in law school (the 1972–73 academic year), I was fortunate to be hired as a law clerk with the Louisiana Department of Justice, Office of the Attorney General, in the Criminal Division. Other law clerks hired with me were Ralph Tyson, whom I had met the summer before at LSU; Graves Thomas, from LSU Law; and Bennie George, a fellow Southern Law School student. We researched legal issues and drafted answers to letters requesting the Attorney General Opinions from state agencies, departments, and political subdivisions to be signed off on by a supervising attorney.

At the end of the school year, Ralph, Graves, and I were offered positions as special counsels in the Criminal Division, contingent upon our passing the July 1973 bar exam. The offer of employment contingent on bar passage was a little sticky. The bar exam is always accompanied by a lot of anxiety, especially for the Southern Law graduates. The school's bar passage rate was low historically, and most students failed on their first attempt. Occasionally, no Southern students passed, and other times only a few would. Most, however, were successful on their second or third try. I was determined to pass the first time I took the exam.

In addition to my own motivation, I had Harriet reminding me she would not accept any excuse for failing the bar exam. She had heard other law students' wives express similar views. Faulting someone else was unacceptable! I had all of the support I needed, but it was up to me to do well.

I studied religiously, taking full advantage of the bar review course offered at LSU. We sat for the exam for three days in July 1973 but had to wait until October to get the results. As the release date approached, I developed a nervous stomach and couldn't hold anything down. With one day remaining, Ralph Tyson and I left the Attorney General's Office to pick up lunch. His car bounced around because its shock absorbers had worn out. Ralph had to stop twice so I could deal with my nervous stomach.

When we got back to the office, we learned that Graves Thomas had called the Louisiana Bar Association and was told he had passed. Graves gave Ralph the bar office's number. He raced upstairs, made a call, and found out he had passed. I then took the number and walked upstairs slowly because my nervous stomach wouldn't permit me to run the way Ralph did. I made the call and found out that I, too, had passed. I sat there for a few minutes to just let the news soak in. What a relief! I called Harriet to tell her. She began to shout, and together we thanked the Lord for the victory. I also called my parents and informed them of my bar passage. It was about twenty minutes before I went back downstairs.

As I walked in, the office staff got quiet. Some of the attorneys were standing around, holding their heads down, assuming that because I had been gone for so long, I didn't pass. "I don't know what you all are looking so sad about," I said. "I passed the bar, and I am going out to celebrate."

I later learned that I was the only one in my class of fifteen students from Southern who passed the exam on the first try. Nonetheless, several of my classmates passed on subsequent attempts and became highly successful and well-respected attorneys.

### Admitted to the Bar

My first job as a lawyer was special counsel, Criminal Division, Office of the Louisiana Attorney General. One of my first assignments was the prosecution of an inmate at the Louisiana State Penitentiary for an attempted escape. Ralph Tyson served as my co-counsel. The venue was the Twentieth Judicial District Court in St. Francisville, Louisiana. This city had a history of being racist and didn't permit African Americans to vote until 1963, and this was 1974. We prepared our case and divided up the witnesses we would examine at the preliminary hearing.

At our first court appearance, we both wore brand-new suits and carried new briefcases. When we entered the courtroom, the judge yelled to the deputy, "Seize those men!" Ralph and I froze in our tracks. Was the judge referring to us? We were there representing the attorney general.

John Sinquefield, our section chief, was already in the courtroom. He stood up and told the judge that we were assistant attorney generals. The judge replied, "They are what?" Sinquefield replied, "They are assistant attorney generals." The judge looked mystified that two Black lawyers were representing the State of Louisiana, but he allowed us to enter the courtroom.

When our case was called, we took our seats at the counsel table on the side usually reserved for the prosecution and immediately observed the judge's continued frustration. In the judge's mind, Ralph and I were in the wrong place. It was apparent that he felt we should have been sitting at the defense table with the Black defendant, and the white attorney representing the defendant should have been seated at the prosecution table. It became clear when we made objections. The judge attributed our objections to the defense instead of to the prosecution. A recess was eventually called, and after that, the judge finally got it right. In the final analysis, our first appearance as bona fide attorneys turned out okay.

My employment with the Criminal Division of the Attorney General's Office turned out to be quite providential. I met several individuals whose careers would greatly influence my path toward a judgeship. We all moved in the same legal circles over the years and benefited from one another's successes. John Sinquefield, Mike Ponder, L. J. Hymel, Ralph Tyson, and I all became assistant district attorneys under District Attorney Ossie Brown in the Nineteenth Judicial District of Louisiana. Kitty Kimball, for whom I clerked during my senior year in law school, and Richard Ieyoub, another Attorney General's Office colleague, became assistant district attorneys (ADAs) in the Eighteenth and Fourteenth Judicial Districts, respectively. These ADA positions proved to be instrumental in our elections to the judiciary. Kitty Kimball became the first woman elected to a judgeship in the Eighteenth Judicial District Court. She was also Louisiana's first female state supreme court justice and its first female chief justice.

Richard Ieyoub went on to become district attorney for Calcasieu Parish, Louisiana, and was later elected attorney general of Louisiana. Michael Ponder was elected to the Baton Rouge City Court and later to the Nineteenth Judicial District Court. L. J. Hymel was elected to the Baton Rouge City Court, the Nineteenth Judicial District Court, and then appointed U.S. attorney for the Middle District of Louisiana. Ralph Tyson was elected to the Baton Rouge City Court and then to the Nineteenth Judicial District Court following me. He was appointed a U.S. District Court judge for the Middle District of Louisiana in 1998. John Sinquefield became chief assistant district attorney under District Attorney Doug Moreau and later first assistant attorney general. I became the first African American elected to the Baton Rouge City Court in 1983, the Nineteenth Judicial District Court in 1987, and the Louisiana First Circuit

Court of Appeal in 1993. After fourteen and a half years in the judiciary I accepted a partnership in the Baton Rouge office of Phelps Dunbar, LLP, an international law firm. In November 2002, I was appointed chancellor/dean of the Southern University Law Center in Baton Rouge.

As I witnessed my former colleagues' successes with elections to judgeships, I raised the question within my own mind, Why not me? Raising the question helped inform my belief that I, too, could be elected to a judgeship. Our résumés and legal experiences were all similar—only the color of our skin differed.

# 2

## Career Path

### *Working the Politics*

W HILE SITTING AT my desk at the Attorney General's Office, I got an unexpected call from City Councilman Joseph Delpit. He wanted to know how I was doing and also congratulated me on passing the bar exam. After a little small talk and catching up on our families, the councilman quickly moved to the reason for his call. He said that the federal aid coordinator job in city-parish government had opened up. He and Councilman Jewel Newman wanted me to apply. I told him that I was satisfied with my position with the Attorney General's Office and wasn't looking to change jobs. He said that if I applied, he could all but assure me I would be selected. Doing so would help him and Councilman Newman place African Americans in upper-level positions in city-parish government.

I wanted more information about the job description, pay scale, and so on. The councilman told me that attorney Glen Ducote had recently resigned from the position. The job involved ensuring that city-parish agencies and departments receiving federal grant funds complied with applicable federal and state grant regulations. Periodic travel to Washington, D.C., to help secure federal funds for various programs and projects also would be required. The pay was a few thousand dollars more than I was making and sounded quite attractive, but I was still reluctant to accept—because of the politics. I didn't see how the job would advance my career as a trial lawyer.

Councilman Delpit emphasized that my background with Community Advancement and my law degree were ideal to sell to the city council. They wanted this position for an African American. After giving it some thought and talking it over with Harriet, I accepted and told Councilman Delpit to close the deal if I could also have a private law practice on the side like Glen Ducote, my predecessor.

The *Morning Advocate* reported that the city council appointed me during a twenty-minute closed-door special council meeting. The article also stated that my predecessor's dissatisfaction with the job was his reason for resigning. Although I was pleased I got the job, reading about Glen Ducote's dissatisfaction with it also gave me a little angst.

The federal-aid position put me in touch with the "movers and shakers" in city government—from the mayor-president to members of the city council, for whom I worked. During my one year's stay on the job, I developed relationships that proved to be quite valuable in later years when running for a judgeship.

Council members would often call on me to research a federal grant for their council district or work with one of their constituents on a local project. Thus, I also developed a close working relationship and friendship with Cleve Taylor, the trusted administrative assistant to Baton Rouge mayor-president Woody Dumas.

Cleve was the one to approach when federal grants were involved. He was a Southern University graduate who had gained considerable experience working with federally sponsored programs. We collaborated on several federal grants for the city. The federal funding that I helped secure and was most proud of was a $500,000 grant for the Capital City Transportation Company (CTC), the bus company's official name at that time. The federal funds enabled the city-parish government to purchase several vans with lifts for wheelchairs.

Probably the most unpleasant part of the job was attending the Wednesday council meetings, which were often full of vitriol and bluster. Certain members took pride in undercutting their colleagues, which made for good press but not good government. Staff members trembled at the thought of having to present before the council, not because they were unprepared but rather because they feared the unprovoked wrath of some uninformed council members.

I learned that the best way to lock down the seven votes needed to pass an item on the council's agenda was to lobby members before the meeting. If you didn't, there would surely be a struggle to get the votes during the meeting. For the most part, I got along with all of the council members. But on one occasion, a particular council member who was also a lawyer with an office not far from mine asked me to come by his office—which I did. He told me that the federal-aid position was a full-time job, and I was not supposed to have a law practice on the side. He suggested that if I sent all of my injury cases to him in a fee-share arrangement, he would not raise the practice issue with the council. I said, "I was following the same rules the council set for Glen Ducote, my predecessor." I asked if he was part of the group of councilmen who voted for me to get this job. He said he wasn't but that he would happily be a part of the group that caused me to lose it. As I got up to leave, I told him that there were some ethical issues involved in this conversation that the Louisiana Bar Association might want to investigate. I left his office and heard no more from him on the subject.

One afternoon I got a call from Mayor Dumas's office asking me to represent him and the council at a National Baptist Association meeting at the Mount Zion Baptist Church that evening. Rev. T. J. Jemison, pastor of Mount Zion and president of the National Baptist Association USA, Inc., listed the mayor and council on its program as delivering greetings. There were several hundred pastors and church members attending from all over the country. I don't remember why neither the mayor nor any council members could make the meeting, but I was happy to oblige. I grew up in the Baptist Church under my great uncle, the Rev. W. M. Pitcher. I knew that I could not approach a church full of Black Baptists with some lofty welcome to our visitors. I had to make a statement that would touch their souls and get the church stirred up and in an "amen" spirit. I proceeded to Mt. Zion, delivered my greeting, and got the rousing response I wanted.

Also on the program that evening was Ossie Brown, district attorney for East Baton Rouge. Ossie had a big, booming voice and was a strong Southern Baptist. He was also proud of his singing ability and thought he would endear himself to the congregation with a song. The song was not all that familiar and didn't have the soul-stirring effect that moved Black Baptists. Ossie offered his greeting and excused himself by saying he had another meeting to attend. I stayed for a few more minutes as the church program slowly moved on. When I got outside, Ossie's driver, Mitch, approached me and said, "Ossie would like to speak to you," and pointed to his vehicle. Ossie told me he liked how I handled myself with that big congregation and then asked if I would like to come to work for him as an assistant district attorney (ADA). I told him that it was an intriguing offer, but I needed to give it some thought. He gave me his card and told me to call him when I was ready to talk.

Although I had worked in the Criminal Division of the Attorney General's Office, I had never thought about becoming an assistant district attorney. I was more focused on establishing my private practice, which was beginning to expand, although I was only working part-time at it. Harriet and I talked and prayed about it, which led me to speak with attorney Van Lacour, one of my mentors. He was dean of Southern University Law School when I started in 1970 and had established a successful civil law practice. Dean Lacour's advice was important and turned out to be very enlightening. He talked about the district attorney's power and authority and the importance of having a Black ADA in that office, which could help stem some of its demonstrated racism. He suggested that I accept the job offer because I had the temperament, wisdom, knowledge, and ability to represent Black folks in that position. I also reached out to Murphy Bell, a highly regarded Black civil rights and criminal defense attorney in Baton Rouge, who agreed with Dean Lacour. He said we needed Black lawyers on both the prosecution side and the defense side of the table. I also called my cousin Alex, who also encouraged me to take the position and saw this as breaking new ground in Baton Rouge. I met with Ossie Brown to follow up on his offer and was hired that same day.

## Assistant District Attorney

Having accepted the assistant district attorney position, I tendered my resignation to the council. My ADA appointment would make me the second Black attorney hired in the East Baton Rouge District Attorney's Office. I was assigned to a Criminal Trial Section in the Nineteenth Judicial District Court. Nathan Wilson, the first Black hired by Ossie, was the chief ADA in East Baton Rouge Juvenile Court. Nathan's position was critical and very important but lacked the visibility you would get from prosecuting cases in the Nineteenth Judicial District Court. That's because juvenile court matters are not open to the public.

I was assigned to work as the misdemeanor assistant in Judge John Covington's court. Lennie Perez was the section chief, and Warren Hebert was the felony assistant. I had a considerable amount of trial experience before taking on the ADA position, thanks to my part-time practice handling DWIs, misdemeanors, and family law matters. I had become pretty adept at defending drug cases, primarily those involving simple possession and possession with intent to distribute marijuana, through motions to suppress. I had been particularly successful in trying suppression motions before Judge Covington. But when I began my tenure as an ADA in Judge Covington's court, it became apparent that he didn't like the move I had made and tried to discourage me by ruling against me in cases I knew I should have won.

Judge Covington would always have a case to cite when he was going to rule against me. So I made it a habit of researching all of the authorities covering the misdemeanor trials I had for a given day and offered distinguishing cases in rebuttal. It was time-consuming, but I was determined not to let him run me off. Things started to change, and I began winning all the misdemeanor cases where I filed bills of information. After I prosecuted the *Walter Monroe* second-degree murder case, the judge asked me to come into his office one morning for a cup of coffee. Drinking coffee with Judge Covington was an experience. He loved to drink from demitasse cups, and his coffee was so thick and strong that you could almost stand a spoon up in it. He told me that he hadn't thought I would last as an ADA, congratulated me on my fortitude, and declared I had made the cut.

Several weeks after Judge Covington's kind declaration, the district attorney called an office-wide meeting and announced a staff realignment. Walter Monsour, the chief executive assistant DA, assigned me to Judge Frank Foil's court, with John Sinquefield as section chief. Doug Moreau and I would share the misdemeanor and felony load. Along with my new assignment came a nice raise. After a couple of months of sharing the felony and misdemeanor in Judge Foil's section, Doug moved on to become the felony assistant in another section of the court, while I assumed full responsibility as the felony assistant in Judge Foil's court.

All ADAs were assigned weeks where they would have to pull duty, which meant that the ADA would assist the police in investigations whenever there was a homicide or rape case. On my first call out, I entered an apartment through a window to observe the deputy coroner, Dr. Louis James, examine a dead person. The decedent had been dead for several days. The stench was horrible, and I nearly threw up. The deceased was sitting on a couch with a .22 pistol in his right hand. He had a can of beer in the other. The bullet wound in his right temple was the cause of death, as determined by the coroner. He also noted that there were no other indications of foul play and ruled the death a suicide.

### State of Louisiana v. James "June" Collins

A weekend duty call that I will never forget occurred on a Saturday morning, November 26, 1976. I received a call that a young Black woman's body had been discovered at about 9:30 a.m. in bushes behind the Five Crown Social Club, a restaurant and bar in Baton Rouge. The young woman suffered a slash from her neck to her pubic area and a stab wound near her neck's base. Blood splatter on a wall and concrete slab at the back of the club indicated she had been mortally wounded near the building and subsequently dragged into the bushes. The victim was found braless, lying on her back, wearing a pair of unbuttoned, unzipped jeans pulled below her hip area. A green sweater was also wrapped around her neck.

Rigor mortis had set in, and ants were crawling over her body, indicating that death had occurred several hours earlier.

I joined the Baton Rouge police officers who investigated the crime. They secured the scene and quickly reconstructed the previous evening's events from information given by some of those present at the nightclub. The victim was eighteen-year-old Karen Jackson. Her boyfriend, Melvin Heard, who worked at the club, identified her body. He worked as a bartender/waiter but occasionally served as manager.

Karen had accompanied her mother, Mrs. Odeal Jackson, and Gloria Francois to the club. They arrived around 9:00 p.m. the Friday night before the discovery of her body. Heard related that he visited with both ladies briefly throughout the night but was called away and was occupied with work the rest of the evening. Gloria visited with friends at another table. I went with detectives to inform Mrs. Jackson of the death of her daughter. This type of visit was a first for me. I wasn't sure how to handle it, so I let the detectives take the lead and provided a shoulder for Mrs. Jackson to cry on. We put her in a car with a police officer to head back to the Five Crown Social Club, where she identified her daughter's body, and then escorted her into the nightclub for questioning. She told us that James Collins had invited himself to sit down with her and Karen. He remained at their table for most of the next two hours, drinking and talking, while Karen ate a hamburger and danced a couple of times. Around 11:30 p.m. Collins told Karen's mother he could score some marijuana for them. Mrs. Jackson declined his offer, but Karen told Collins she would accept. He left the table briefly and returned, stating that he had gotten some marijuana for her from a friend. Karen left her food, coat, and purse at the table with her mother and went outside with Collins. They left by the front door, which opened onto a heavily traveled city street. A drizzling rain, which had begun earlier and would continue through the night, was still falling at the time she left the table. Karen was never seen alive again by her mother or any other folks at the nightclub after leaving with Collins. Collins did not come back into the club, but when Melvin Heard locked up at 2:00 a.m., he saw Collins talking with a man and his daughter out in front of the building.

Based upon what Karen's mother and Melvin Heard told them, along with their findings at the crime scene, the police sought out James Collins for questioning. As they emerged from the Five Crown Social Club, one of the officers who knew Collins saw him in front of the B & P Club a half block down the street. Collins saw the officers and swiftly walked into the B & P Club as if to avoid them. However, the officers quickly removed Collins from the club and took him downtown to the police headquarters for questioning. During the interrogation, the police discovered what appeared to be blood on his shoes and under his fingernails. The state police crime lab criminalist took fingernail scrapings from Collins and his shoes to analyze them. The criminalist worked all day Sunday and handed in a preliminary report on Monday confirming that the bloodstains on Collins's shoes matched the victim's rare blood type. When the officers questioned Collins about the dark coloring under his fingernails, he said it came from eating barbecue the previous night. The crime lab proved the scrapings from his fingernails were human blood, not animal blood.

Armed with the blood evidence, I brought the evidence before the grand jury for an indictment of first-degree murder. This indictment would mark the first such indictment in Baton Rouge since the U.S. Supreme Court reinstated the death penalty with its 1972 decision in *Furman v. Georgia*. Since I was the duty assistant who worked the case, I argued against attempting to hand off the case to a more senior ADA. Although I was only three years out of law school, I felt that I could handle it, and I wanted to do so. The murder occurred in the Black community, and I wanted to speak up for the community with this prosecution. The district attorney agreed, and I proceeded to prepare the case for trial. Karen's murder occurred in the same neighborhood where Collins had committed his first murder. He had been convicted of second-degree murder and had served more than ten years in the Louisiana State Penitentiary at Angola for bludgeoning the father of Dr. Emmett Bashful, a Southern University administrator, to death. The general sentiment I gathered was that folks in the neighborhood wanted him gone once and for all.

The Louisiana Legislature amended the statutory definition of first-degree murder and added Code of Criminal Procedure Articles 905.4 and 905.5 in 1976, which introduced aggravating and mitigating circumstances that a jury must consider before imposing the death penalty. Their action was in response to the U.S. Supreme Court's decision in *Furman v. Georgia* and *Roberts v. Louisiana*, bifurcating a first-degree murder trial into a guilt phase and penalty phase. In the trial's guilt phase, the state has to prove every essential element of the crime of first-degree murder as statutorily defined. In the penalty phase, the state must prove, and the jury must find, at least one or more of seven statutory aggravating circumstances before imposing the death penalty. The jury must also consider one or more of seven mitigating circumstances and an eighth catchall provision: "Any other relevant mitigating circumstance. In a death penalty case, the jury must unanimously agree; otherwise, the sentence is life imprisonment without benefit of probation, parole, or suspension of sentence."

Although I was somewhat ambivalent about my belief in the death penalty, I chose to pursue an indictment for first-degree murder after reviewing the aggravating circumstances under Code of Criminal Procedure Article 905.4. Three of the seven aggravating circumstances fit perfectly:

1. The killing occurred during the perpetration or attempted perpetration of aggravated rape.
2. The offender has been previously convicted of an unrelated murder.
3. The offense was committed in an especially heinous, atrocious, or cruel manner.

The brutality inflicted upon this young girl's body was so reprehensible that I felt he should answer with his own life.

After Collins's arrest, Judge Foil appointed two well-qualified attorneys to represent him. Dennis Whalen, a highly respected criminal defense lawyer, was lead, and John Samaha was co-counsel and second chair. Dennis and John launched a vigorous defense, filing all of the appropriate motions one would expect in a case of this magnitude. Defending against a barrage of pretrial motions and preparing for the trial represented a tremendous task. I was able to lean on John Sinquefield, my section chief, and several top-notch DA investigators to help me assemble and organize the case for trial. The cooperation and assistance of the detectives and uniformed police officers who worked the case undergirded my efforts.

I called a series of meetings to review the evidence and to lock down the chain of custody for all of the evidence gathered at the scene. I created a detailed chart that listed every piece of evidence with every person's name who handled it, from gathering it to marking and filing it into the evidence room.

An essential aspect of a first-degree murder trial is the impaneling of the so-called death-qualified jury. A death-qualified jury means that no juror is categorically opposed to capital punishment or believes that the death penalty must be imposed in all instances of capital murder.

Once the trial began, we worked late into the evening, finally selecting the first juror around 6:00 p.m. That juror was immediately sequestered and put up in a hotel until a full complement of jurors and alternates was selected. It took three more days to select the remaining jurors, again requiring us to work late into the evening. The process was grueling, and you could see the toll it was taking on members of the jury venire as we questioned each one. The actual trial only lasted about four days. Judge Foil pushed us late into the evening, granting periodic recesses for meals or coffee breaks.

The *Collins* trial was a high-profile murder case, not because of who the victim or defendant was, but because it was the first death penalty case in Baton Rouge since its reinstitution by the U.S. Supreme Court. Both print and broadcast coverage were widespread. Deputy Coroner Dr. Louis James testified as to the cause of death, having performed the autopsy on the victim. He declared that a bloody brickbat was not the murder weapon, which caused a reporter to run out and feed that line to his paper, which made it part of the headlines the following day. Had they stayed around into the night, reporters would have gotten a better picture of the evidence as it unfolded and would have learned what weapon had brought about the victim's death.

I introduced well more than one hundred items into evidence during the trial. But the most consequential of all was the blood evidence gathered from the defendant's shoes, clothing, and fingernails. A gas chromatography–mass spectrometer was used to determine the victim's blood type, which was broken down into subtypes, matching the victim's blood to the blood found on Collins's clothing, shoes, and fingernails. This blood typing back then was an ancient process compared to the DNA testing we have today.

The case continued into the weekend. On Sunday afternoon, the jury returned a unanimous verdict of guilty of first-degree murder. As the clerk read the verdict and as the jury was polled, I could tell this trial had taken a tremendous toll on several of the female jurors. Given the emotional impact the evidence had upon these jurors during the trial's guilt phase, I thought those emotions might prove problematic for them in the trial's penalty phase, when the decision was life or death.

Spectators packed the courtroom daily through to the final verdict. Instead of thanking the jury for their service and dismissing them, Judge Foil advised them to remain under sequestration and return to court the following day to begin the second phase of the trial, called the penalty phase. District Attorney Brown; Walter Monsour, his first assistant; and my section chief, John Sinquefield, were all in the courtroom when the jury returned the guilty verdict. They heartily congratulated me, as did the detectives and police officers who worked the case. Initially, the police thought that the packed courtroom was full of Collins's supporters and wanted to escort me across the street to the DA's office. I assured them that the folks there just wanted to see that Karen got the justice she deserved.

After the jury left the courtroom, I gathered my materials and returned to my office across the street. Ossie invited me to his office for a postmortem. He congratulated me on the conviction and suggested that Ralph Roy, the most senior ADA on staff, help me with the penalty phase the following afternoon. I objected to having Ralph get involved at this point. I pointed out that the jury was already on the edge of breaking because of the decision before them, and Ralph's style might overwhelm them.

Though Ralph was the most senior prosecutor in the office, he never offered me any advice or assistance, nor did he ever ask how things were going. I told Ossie I was prepared for the penalty phase and didn't need any help. With that, he let me continue on my own.

Even if the jury decided not to impose the death penalty, I had already accomplished what I wanted, which was to get a conviction of first-degree murder. At minimum, James "June" Collins would be incarcerated for the remainder of his life. My goal was to present the evidence and leave it up to the jury to determine his fate. I offered little opposition to the mitigating circumstances.

I could see that this experience shook the jury to its core. Several of the women on the jury were crying. All they wanted to do was to get out of there and go home. The judge asked the foreman if they had reached a verdict, and he replied they had.

The verdict was not to impose the death penalty. Again, I was satisfied that James "June" Collins would pay for the murder of eighteen-year-old Karen Jackson by spending the rest of his life in prison without the benefit of parole, probation, or suspension of his sentence.

## Full-Time Private Practice

Not long after the *Collins* case, I decided to go into private practice full-time. One of the last cases I prosecuted involved a charge of felony theft by fraud. The defendant had endeared himself to an elderly Black woman and gotten her to empty her savings account on the pretense that he would double her money. When she realized that she was the victim of a scam, or "pigeon drop," the perpetrator was long gone. He was subsequently apprehended in Mississippi and extradited to Louisiana for trial in Baton Rouge. I got the case and filed a bill of information charging him with felony theft. The defendant, who had bonded out of jail, appeared in court wearing dark glasses. He was being led by the hand of a little boy. We picked a jury and began putting on evidence.

My victim was very high-strung and hard to control. She was so angry that she wanted to tell the court everything she knew about the man who had defrauded her and was not responsive to my questions. During my witness preparation, I had shared with her that the defendant had a long rap sheet dating back several years and had served time in prison. She took it upon herself to tell the jury about his convictions rather than answer the questions I asked. Of course, the defense counsel objected and moved for a mistrial, which the court granted. A new trial date was selected, but I had no intention of being around for a second trial.

I resumed my plan to return to private practice, as I had accomplished all I wanted to in the two and a half years I was an ADA. I had tried more than a hundred misdemeanor cases and more than two dozen felony jury cases, ranging from felony theft to first-degree murder. In between were multiple motions to suppress, preliminary examinations, and even an oral argument before the Louisiana Supreme Court. When I wasn't trying cases myself, I observed other ADAs prosecuting cases and picked up trial tactics and practice pointers. My move to private practice was not just about having a criminal law practice. The skill set I acquired as an ADA was transferrable to the civil court since both prosecutors and plaintiff attorneys have to prove their cases by direct evidence.

I was on the front porch of my office at 2024 Plank Road one morning, getting out my key to unlock the door, when a brand-new Cadillac swerved into the parking lot of my building. The defendant I had prosecuted several weeks ago in the "theft by fraud" case, who supposedly was blind, was driving the car. Baffled as to why he was at my office, I quickly wanted to know what he wanted. He told me he had fired his lawyer and tried to hire me. I politely told him that it would be a conflict of interest for me to take his case, that the district attorney would surely object, and that the judge would never let me change sides. With that, I showed him to the door!

Once I was back in private practice full-time, I enticed Carolyn Ricks to give up her job at Community Advancement, Inc., and come back to work for me full-time. Working for me full-time, however, also meant that she would be working for the other attorneys in the office. Soon it became necessary to hire another full-time secretary, so we hired Monica O'Connor.

At this point I was the only one in the office who practiced full-time. Ralph left the District Attorney's Office and accepted the city prosecutor's position for the Baton Rouge City Court. Don Avery was the full-time pastor of Neely Methodist Church; Edselle Cunningham and Tim Hardy were employed full-time with the Attorney General's Office. With my full-time practice and their part-time practices, our office stayed quite busy. Although we maintained our separate law practices, we operated as partners in a law firm, often sharing cases and making court appearances for one another.

## High-Profile Cases

Although I maintained a part-time civil practice while in the District Attorney's Office, moving into a full-time practice was a serious gamble. Solo practitioners wondered if they could attract a client base strong enough to sustain them financially. In those days, lawyers were precluded from advertising and relied primarily on client referrals and reputations to draw new clients. Handling high-profile cases that got newspaper coverage always helped get new clients in the door. Shortly after leaving the District Attorney's Office, I picked up two such cases. The first was the *State of Louisiana v. Sanford Hawkins*. Sanford was the superintendent of the Louisiana Training Institute for Boys (LTI). He was indicted in East Baton Rouge on two counts of perjury before the grand jury and three counts of cruelty to juveniles. The second case was the *United States of America v. Lee Wesley*. Lee was the executive director of Community Advancement, Inc., the local antipoverty program, a close friend. A federal grand jury had indicted him for conspiracy to misapply federal funds and four counts of the substantive offense of misapplication. I was the second chair in Lee's case, assisting Jim McPherson, a well-known criminal defense lawyer from New Orleans. Jim had a reputation for handling high-profile cases in federal courts throughout the state and around the South.

In the *Hawkins* case, Sanford allegedly locked three young teen escapees from LTI in the trunk of his car while he chased down several other boys who were still on the run. When called before the grand jury, he allegedly lied on two separate occasions, resulting in the two perjury counts. As I began my discovery, I was provided the transcript of his first appearance but advised that there was no transcript of his second appearance because the recording equipment supposedly had malfunctioned. He allegedly perjured himself on each occasion. By law, I was entitled to a transcription of the portion of the grand jury testimony that evidenced the perjury. Therefore, I quickly moved to quash one count of the indictment because the state could not produce my client's allegedly perjured testimony. Judge Elmore Lear, the trial judge on the case, ruled that the state still had a right to put on a case despite the malfunctioning equipment. He suggested that the state might want to call the grand jury members to testify.

I again moved to quash the indictment because there was no credible evidence of perjury to substantiate the prosecution's charge and subpoenaed the entire grand jury. I wanted to test the grand jury's recollection of the questions asked and my client's answers. Just as I surmised, none of them had any recollection of his testimony. The judge subsequently agreed to grant my motion to quash that perjury count. I then turned my attention to the second count of perjury, contending that the question and answer that led to it were not, under the law, material to prosecute cruelty to juveniles. The judge took my argument under advisement and deferred his ruling to the trial of the case.

Warren Hebert, the assistant district attorney handling this case, was one of my supervisors when I was in the DA's Office. When Judge Lear made a favorable ruling in my case, he appeared unable to contain his annoyance. I believed the case was better suited for trial before the judge and had Sanford waive trial before a jury.

My goal was to demonstrate that being locked in Sanford's trunk for a few minutes did not rise to a level of harm contemplated by the statute that defined cruelty to juveniles. As I had surmised, each one on cross-examination wanted to show how tough he was and told the court that being locked in the trunk of the car "was no big deal." Warren was doing all he could to control the boys but to no avail. He finally rested his case, and the judge recessed the trial until after lunch. During that recess, I reviewed my trial notes, and I noticed that Warren had failed to prove each of the alleged victims' ages.

When the court reconvened, I moved for a directed verdict of acquittal because the state failed to prove that the victims were juveniles. Warren quickly moved to reopen his case in chief, to which I strongly objected. I argued that the state should not have two bites at the apple to prove its case. He had a chance to present his evidence in his case in chief but failed to do so. The judge denied his motion and granted mine for a directed verdict. One count of perjury remained, and he had taken that under advisement. The judge ultimately ruled that the question posed and answer given were not material to the prosecution of the charge of cruelty to juveniles, adopting the argument I made at the outset, and granted my motion to quash. The judge's ruling, in this case, was a big victory. The trial drew both print and broadcast coverage, turning out to be a PR bonanza. My subpoena of the grand jury was a bold move that attracted a lot of attention. The *Hawkins* case certainly raised my profile in the criminal defense bar.

My involvement in the *United States of America v. Lee Wesley* case also received a great deal of media coverage. That case involved interpreting federal procurement law and rules and the regulations of the U.S. Community Service Administration—the federal agency that oversaw community action agencies around the country. The government contended that Lee Wesley, the executive director of Community Advancement, Inc., and Kent Smith, the assistant director, gave preferential no-bid contracts for goods and services to a friend in violation of federal law. However, there was never an allegation that either received any personal benefit from these transactions. Lee was a friend of mine from both high school and my job with Community Advancement, Inc., and I very much wanted to see him through this ordeal. As the trial date neared, lead counsel Jim McPherson and I thought we needed to get someone from the Federal Community Services Administration (CSA) in Washington to serve as an expert witness on its procurement laws. That required me to cut through the red tape and go straight to the Community Services Administration's secretary.

I turned to my friend State Representative Joe Delpit. He arranged a meeting for me with Governor Edwin Edwards, who agreed to make the call. I flew to Washington, D.C., the next day and contacted a top CSA employee, who assigned a procurement expert to hear me out. The expert agreed with our interpretation of the procurement regulations on several charges but was less convinced about one of the transactions. We decided to subpoena his testimony anyway.

We arranged for the procurement expert's transportation and hotel accommodations. He was to contact me upon arrival. The day before the trial, I waited anxiously for his call. Finally, late into the evening, I heard from him. He told me that he had been picked up at the airport by the FBI and taken downtown. They questioned him for several hours regarding the nature of his testimony. He was considerably shaken by the experience. Given the situation, we decided not to call him and instead call someone from the regional office of CSA out of Dallas to give an opinion on the procurement laws and regulations in question. The expert was a critical part of our defense. Realizing the battleground and the stakes, the U.S. Attorney's Office apparently had me surveilled when I made my trip to Washington, D.C. That's the only way the FBI would have known about our witness from the CSA.

The trial lasted for several days. The jury convicted both Lee and Kent Smith on all counts. Before sentencing, we filed a motion to set aside the conviction on the grounds of prosecutorial misconduct. In his closing argument, Don Beckner, the U.S. attorney, made several egregious and inflammatory statements to the jury that did not comport with either the law or evidence in the case.

On the day of sentencing, Judge E. Gordon West took our motion up first. He stated that in more than twenty years on the federal bench, he had never set aside or vacated a jury's verdict. He then told a packed courtroom that, in this case, however, he agreed with the defense motion that prosecutorial misconduct had occurred during the closing argument and then granted our motion. There was an outburst of joy and jubilation by friends and supporters of Lee and Kent. But the judge's ruling also meant we had to do this all over again. Due to the overabundance of trial publicity, we filed for a change of venue, which the judge granted.

The trial was moved to Lake Charles for trial before Judge Edwin Hunter. Unfortunately, Lee and Kent were again convicted. However, Judge Hunter noted that he did not think much of the case and sentenced both Lee and Kent to a period of supervised probation, with no jail time ordered or deferred. The case proved to be another boost for my practice. Both Lee and Kent were able to resume their lives and regain their status as upstanding citizens in the Baton Rouge community. Most folks acknowledged that their ordeal was a by-product of local politics.

# 3

# The Phone Call That Started It All

O N A MONDAY MORNING in the middle of September 1982, Carolyn Ricks, my secretary, buzzed me that Bill Weatherford was on the phone. He called to tell me that L. J. Hymel was planning to run for Frank Foil's seat on the district court, and when Foil moved up to the First Circuit, he planned to run for Hymel's seat on the city court. Bill asked for my support, and without any hesitation, I told Bill I couldn't support him because I was also planning to run. I assumed he had heard some gossip and was hoping to head me off. I had attended a couple of campaign functions for L. J. Hymel as he was gearing up to run for the Nineteenth Judicial District Court and had let a few folks know that I was considering running for the city court seat upon L. J.'s election to the district court.

I had thought about running before but had not seriously discussed it with anyone but my wife. I now had to decide if running for a judgeship is what I truly wanted to do. My practice was expanding. Sidney Hall and I had recently won a wrongful death case against the State of Louisiana and earned a rather large fee. I had also settled another lawsuit against the state involving an inmate raping a nurse at the Feliciana Forensic Facility. My client base had steadily increased on both the criminal and civil sides, and I had to decide if I wanted to give all of that up.

As I saw it, running for the city court would not hinge on my qualifications. The primary issue would be about race and whether Baton Rouge was ready to elect its first Black judge. I believed I was well qualified for the position. I had many of the same experiences that others used to help them get elected. The Louisiana Supreme Court had appointed me to a brief stint on the Baton Rouge City Court as an ad hoc judge. I had been an assistant district attorney for the Parish of East Baton Rouge and a special counsel in the Criminal Division of the Louisiana Attorney General's Office. I headed an up-and-coming law firm, Pitcher, Tyson, Avery, and Cunningham. I had a strong litigation background, having prosecuted the first capital murder trial in Baton Rouge after the U.S. Supreme Court decision in *Furman v. Georgia.* I graduated in the top 10 percent of my law school class and passed the bar exam on my first attempt. I felt my credentials made me a strong candidate. But no Black judicial candidate had successfully been elected to the bench in Baton Rouge in several attempts.

Like the game of musical chairs, moving from court to court played out in Baton Rouge for years. The most significant battles were between judges sitting on the same bench deciding whose turn it was to move up. A judge staking a claim to a vacant higher seat would generally move up without opposition. Bill and I were about to square off for an open city court judgeship, contingent upon Judge Foil moving up to the Louisiana First Court of Appeal and L. J. Hymel moving up from city court to the Nineteenth Judicial District Court to replace him. Although several Black lawyers had attempted to break the judicial glass ceiling in Baton Rouge, to date, none had been successful.

I recall a letter I received from Rev. Ulysses Hayes, president of the First Ward Voters League, in which he urged me to run for city judge. The League had reviewed a list of Black lawyers and determined that I was the best candidate to take up the mantle. I thought about a conversation I had with Judge Lewis Doherty during which he encouraged me to consider running for city court. He called one day after taking a case I tried before him under advisement, and he told me I was among the top of the many young trial lawyers who had tried cases before him. He then asked if I ever considered running for a city court judgeship. I was flattered by his assessment of my skills and encouraged by his interest in my potential candidacy. He also advised that I had won my redhibition case.

I had discussed a run for the city court with Harriet several years earlier, after receiving the letter from Rev. Ulysses Hayes suggesting that I consider making a run for a city court judgeship. Harriet told me she did not think the time was right. I drove home, wondering what Harriet would say about Bill Weatherford's call and what I told him. Expecting pushback, I was surprised when she wholeheartedly encouraged me to run! Having Harriet's support sealed my decision to mount a campaign for the Baton Rouge City Court.

Throughout our marriage, Harriet listened to me express my dreams and aspirations and was always insightful in her responses. When I lost my focus on going to law school, Harriet steered me back on course. She has been there with me from the start, encouraging, supporting, and grounding me. I valued her counsel.

Harriet was an accomplished politician in her own right. She was elected to several local and national offices with the National Association of Bench and Bar Spouses (NABBS, Inc.), an affiliate of the National Bar Association. She was president of the Baton Rouge chapter of Jack and Jill of America. The relationships that she developed through her civic engagement and our church affiliation would prove extremely valuable during my campaign. Her warm, engaging personality and her charm attracted many of her friends and associates to our effort, especially during crunch times when stuffing envelopes and making calls from our phone bank were critical.

Harriet was a speech and hearing therapist and employed by the East Baton Rouge Parish School System. She offered to write a letter soliciting support for my election from all the teachers in the system. David Roach, my political consultant, offered to write the letter, but Harriet wanted to write it herself and did. Harriet pulled off a rather remarkable feat when she arranged for the letter to be distributed to teachers via the school system's interagency mail system, called the Pony. That was a big deal and a big money saver.

I also needed the five attorneys in my office to support my campaign. Even though we were not a law firm per se, we held ourselves out as one. We used joint stationery with the heading Pitcher, Tyson, Avery, and Cunningham. Tim Hardy and Elaine Boyle were associates, and their names were on our letterhead too. We were often called the "Plank

Road boys," a moniker that stuck even after Elaine joined the office. As a group, we were steadily building a positive reputation in the community.

I asked everyone in the office to join me in our conference room and told them I had decided to run for a seat on the Baton Rouge City Court. Ralph (Tyson), Don (Avery), Edselle (Cunningham), Tim (Hardy), and Elaine were all very supportive. I told them that there could be only one Black candidate in the race for my campaign to be successful. Therefore, I had to preemptively move to solidify support before another Black lawyer decided that he or she wanted to run. The place to start was at the upcoming meeting of the Louis A. Martinet Society, the Black bar association in Baton Rouge.

At the Martinet meeting I asked for the floor and told the members of my telephone conversation with Bill Weatherford and my decision to run for the next open seat on the Baton Rouge City Court. I told them I decided to run because it was long overdue for the city to have a Black judge.

In 1978, Walter Dumas was appointed judge ad hoc and became the first Black to serve on the Baton Rouge City Court. He later ran but did not make the runoff in a four-person race that included Robert Eames, another Black attorney. The eventual winner was Judge William Brown. Dumas and Eames effectively eliminated each other in the primary.

That same year, Norbert Rayford ran against Doug Moreau, a former LSU football star, and lost by a mere two thousand votes. His vote total was encouraging, considering Baton Rouge's demographics and Doug's name recognition from his LSU football days. I told the group that if Mr. Rayford wanted to make another run, I would step aside for him.

I wanted to know if any Martinet members other than me had planned to become a candidate. Not hearing anyone speak up, I told them I assumed that I would be the only Black candidate in the race and asked for their votes and support. Though I got the rousing show of support from the members I was looking for, there were some naysayers. Several members thought that my run would be an exercise in futility. Despite the city's history of racial segregation and discrimination, which was evident in the city's voting patterns, I thought the timing was right to crack the judicial glass ceiling.

I was beginning to acquire some of the trappings of success: a home in Concord Estates, a brand-new 280 SE Mercedes-Benz, and money in the bank. With all of the excitement swirling around the prospect of running for a judgeship, I never considered a city court judge's salary. When I found out about the pay, it gave me a pause, as I was making considerably more money in private practice. Nevertheless, I would not change my mind at this point. It was a civil rights issue for me. It was time to have Black representation on the bench in Baton Rouge, and I was determined to be the one to provide it. I always wanted to contribute to the struggle for civil rights and justice in a meaningful way. Breaking down this barrier was one way I could make a significant contribution.

The news of my decision to run was spreading. About two weeks after my initial conversation with Bill Weatherford, I got a call from James "Jim" Boren, an attorney I knew from my time in the District Attorney's Office. Jim was the chief appellant assistant. He invited me to join him and one of his partners for lunch at the City Club.

I arrived there the next day and was ushered to a table in a side room in the Men's Grill to join Jim and Frank Holthaus. After we ordered, Jim began talking about the city court seat. He said Bob Downing, a close friend of his, had also planned to run. He suggested that we should not run against one another. If I deferred to Bob in this election, they would support me for the next open seat. I told them I had a counterproposal, you support me on this one, and I'll support Bob on the next one. I then said that there were no Black judges on either the city or district bench, and it was about time for the situation to change. I was committed to running, and I told them I was not about to wait any longer.

I ran into Bob Downing in front of a drugstore on College Drive a few days later. To my surprise, he handed me a check for one hundred dollars payable to my campaign fund and said he had given the race some thought and decided against running. He told me he would support me and suggested that I contact David Roach, a political consultant who could help with my campaign.

Besides my personal belief that I could mount a successful judicial campaign, I had no hard-and-fast evidence regarding demographics. I believed that I could get more than seven thousand votes. That was the number of votes that Byron Stringer had received in the most recent city court election. Following Bob Downing's advice, I gave David a call.

David came over to my office on Plank Road. He brought a stack of papers, including computer printouts and campaign materials from various races he had worked on over the years. Though a longtime friend of Bob Downing's, David felt it was a less opportune time for him to run than for me. David believed my reputation in the legal community was strong enough to help me win a city court race based upon some research he had done, even though African Americans made up only 40 percent of the city's voters at the time.

David had worked on political campaigns for several years and had developed expertise in polling and analyzing voter turnout. He had also developed a reputation as a flamethrower who cranked out negative campaign ads that reflected poorly on opponents. David started working for Congressman Gillis Long when he was contemplating running for governor a second time. He had studied and analyzed the last ten years of special elections in Baton Rouge. Voter turnout for single-ballot issues was his focus. He found that Black voter turnout averaged around 8 percent, whereas white voter turnout averaged around 10 percent. "So, it's about the arithmetic," he said. My job was to energize Black voters to get to the polls at a much higher percentage than in previous elections. At the same time, I needed to get 15 percent of the white vote to win. I now had more than an anecdotal theory on my side, which would help me garner support from leaders in the Black community.

Based upon past data, L. J. Hymel's election to the district court seemed inevitable. That being the case, I needed to gin up some early support. The place to begin was at the Chicken Shack, the South Baton Rouge Advisory Council's unofficial political headquarters. I bumped into the Council's chairman there and told him of my intentions, asking how I could get the Council's support. He wanted to know if there was currently a vacant seat. I had to tell him no, but one would likely be open soon. He told me we could talk then.

I also tried reaching out to Rev. T. J. Jemison of Mt. Zion First Baptist Church. In addition to his pastorate, Reverend Jemison was also the president of the National Baptist Convention, USA, Inc., and a leading figure in Baton Rouge and around the state and nation. Reverend Jemison led the historic Baton Rouge bus boycott of 1953 that served as the road map for the famous Montgomery bus boycott that Dr. Martin Luther King led in 1955. Unfortunately, Reverend Jemison had no time for me and suggested I come back later.

I was having lunch at the Chicken Shack one day when I was joined at the table by a gentleman who identified himself as a minister of the Gospel. He said that he pastored a church in West Baton Rouge. As we talked, I told him I planned to run for a judgeship on the Baton Rouge City Court. I laid out the scenario of how the seat would come about and why, and that I believed I could win. I told him that my quest for support from local leaders was progressing slowly. He tore off a piece of cardboard and wrote three scriptures down for me to read daily, telling me they would help me find my bearings.

The scriptures were:

Exodus 14:14: "The Lord will fight for you; you need only be still";

Luke 10:19: "Behold, I give unto you power to tread on serpents and scorpions, and over all the power of the enemy: and nothing shall by any means hurt you"; and

Romans 8:31: "What then can we say to these things? If God be for us, who can be against us?"

As I began to read the scriptures, a calmness came over me, and I felt reenergized. Until the race for the city court was called, I realized that I had many things I needed to do to enhance my candidacy.

## The Black Church

I knew that I needed to get Black political leaders and their organizations' support to mount a successful campaign from the very start. Equally important was garnering the help and support of the Black church community. I grew up in the Sixty Aid Baptist Church in Baton Rouge, pastored by my great-uncle, Rev. W. M. Pitcher. I knew the church to be an excellent place to mobilize Black voters, find campaign workers, and enlist community organizers. As a young boy I witnessed firsthand how white politicians courted the Black vote. Whenever a white person showed up on a Sunday morning, we all knew that there had to be an election at hand. That was not the case for me. I was from and of the Black community and just a phone call away.

I sought out Rev. Ulysses Hayes first since his letter played a significant role in my decision to run. He enthusiastically endorsed my candidacy and reminded me of the letter he wrote to me some time back, encouraging me to run. I then sought the support of Rev. Lionel Lee, pastor of the Shady Grove Missionary Baptist Church, an activist in the Black community, and editor of the *Weekly Press*. Securing Reverend Lee's support, I contacted Rev. Charles Smith, pastor of Shiloh Missionary Baptist Church, one of the largest Black churches in Baton Rouge. I knew these men were politically active, and their endorsements and support were crucial to creating a groundswell in the church community. After I met with them, they agreed to join Reverend Hayes on a Church Steering Committee and help my campaign.

The first meeting of the Church Steering Committee took place at the Shiloh Missionary Baptist Church. I explained our strategy and how Black churches played a significant role. I was running in a special election with expected low voter turnout. I explained that the judge who won the last city court special election got into office with little more than seven thousand votes. I told them I needed to get more than seven thousand votes. My goal was to have the Black voter turnout outpace the white voter turnout percentage-wise. This strategy meant that we had to ignite a passion in the Black community like the one that fueled the civil rights marches of the 1960s. I wanted to start by meeting with a large group of church pastors to solicit their help. Reverend Lee suggested that the best way to reach the Black clergy in a large gathering was at a prayer breakfast. We decided to kick-start our strategy by inviting all the Black pastors in Baton Rouge. Reverend Smith offered to host the breakfast at Shiloh. Reverends Lee and Hayes helped me put together the list of invitees. More than one hundred pastors, associate pastors, and assistant pastors received invitations. I was a deacon at Belfair Baptist Church and the great-nephew of Rev. W. M. Pitcher and Rev. Alex Pitcher. Reverend W. M. was president of the Emanuel Aid Baptist Association. These connections I felt significantly enhanced my standing within the Baptist church community.

Although I didn't get a chance to meet with Reverend Jemison as I had hoped, I got an enormous endorsement statement from him one Sunday morning during his regular Sunday church radio broadcast. He told his congregation and the listening audience that he was impressed with what he had seen with my campaign, billboards, and yard signs, popping up all over the city, and all professionally done. He said that I even looked like a judge. When I visited his church, he urged his members to vote for me and contribute to my campaign.

# 4

# Running for Judge and Challenges

I T WAS NOW OFFICIAL: L. J. Hymel was the new district court judge. His city seat was open, and a qualifying date and an election date were called to fill the vacancy. I made it a point to be the first to file and was at the clerk of court's office with qualifying papers and filing fee in hand before the doors opened. I wanted to demonstrate that I was ready to run and didn't want anyone to question that conviction. I knew Bill Weatherford was going to file but was surprised when a third candidate entered the race on the last day of qualifying. Ronald DeFrances, who had recently moved to the city, also filed to run. However, the parish attorney challenged his candidacy because he did not meet the residency requirement to run for city court judge. Under state law, a city court candidate had to be a city resident for two years. DeFrances contended that the city charter, which did not delineate a specific length of time to determine residency, should control, rather than state law.

The city was joined in its suit against DeFrances by Pete DeWeese, who claimed to be a concerned citizen. We all assumed that he was acting on behalf of Bill Weatherford. With DeFrances out of the race, the primary became our general election. Bill thought that getting DeFrances out of the race would work to his benefit because he wouldn't have to split the white vote, putting the demographics squarely in his favor. But strategically, I believed DeFrances's departure increased my chances of winning. I no longer had to worry about voter falloff after a primary. There would only be a general election.

My campaign kickoff event involved a DJ from the WXOK radio station. Periodically throughout the day, I went live on the radio to announce my candidacy. In thirty- to forty-five-second sound bites, I squeezed in as much information about myself as possible. We invited radio listeners to stop by, grab a hot dog, and pick up a "Fred Pitcher for City Judge" yard sign. People stopped by all day. Since my campaign headquarters was in my office, this event was also beneficial for business, as Ralph and the other lawyers in the office can attest.

Unexpected visitors to our campaign event were the Zumo brothers, Raymond and Frankie. I had met them at one of L. J. Hymel's fundraising events. L. J. had acknowledged my presence to his audience and announced that I planned to run for his seat upon his election to the district court. L. J.'s statement boosted my campaign prospects because 95 percent of the people in his audience were white. Frankie Zumo came over, introduced himself, and asked if he could help with my campaign. I took his number and said I would give him a call. Before I had a chance to call him, he and Raymond showed up at my kickoff event. The brothers were both pipefitters and worked for UA Local 198 Plumbers & Steamfitters. Raymond was a union steward. They gathered up a number of my yard signs and invited me to the union hall to make a pitch for my election. Both Raymond and Frankie became stalwarts in my election efforts. They arranged to have my campaign yard signs strategically placed in the white community, attended all of my events, and spearheaded the effort to get me their union's endorsement.

I needed to establish a support group of family and friends who could serve as my eyes and ears in the community and help thwart any problems that might crop up during the campaign. Although my father was a voracious reader of the newspaper and kept abreast of most political issues, I had to explain in detail to him what our strategy was and what we needed to do to make it work. My dad was on board, but I knew that getting others on board would not be as easy.

The second and most important reason for sitting down with my dad was to explain what lay ahead. Since his retirement, Dad had become a heavy drinker. He needed to know that my candidacy would put the entire family in the spotlight and that his conduct would reflect on my campaign. Harriet and I once hosted a campaign function at our home for U.S. Senator Russell Long attended by fifty to seventy-five people in a patio and backyard event. Dad had a lot to drink that evening and wanted to ask Senator Long a question. I could tell he was agitated, and I knew his question would be contentious. Not wanting him to create a scene, I quickly ushered him into the house and away from the crowd on the patio. My father said he wanted to take Senator Long to task for some political position he had taken that adversely affected Black folks. His question might have been legitimate, but he was not in a condition to ask it. Hosting this event was politically important for me and our neighborhood, and had I not intervened with my dad when I did, Harriet and I would have suffered great embarrassment. Our conversation seemed to have done some good because my dad curbed his drinking for the remainder of the campaign.

## Building a Campaign Team

One Sunday I started writing down names to contact of those within both the Black and white communities who could support my campaign financially. I needed to reach out to the Black leaders in Baton Rouge, beginning with Joseph Delpit, now a state representative. Although he was not the South Baton Rouge Advisory Council chairman, Delpit was the driving force behind it. I also needed to reach out to Rev. Ulysses Hayes of the First Ward Voters League; Louis Jetson, who was with the Gus Young Civic Association; State Senator Richard "Dick" Turnley, a member of the Scotlandville Advisory Council; and Acie Belton of the Second Ward Voters League. There were also about ten smaller political groups I needed to court, but locking down the "big five" was of paramount importance.

The smaller political groups were generally started by individuals who had become disaffected with one or more of the "big five" and sought to become power brokers in their own right. White politicians often used them as foils when they did not receive the support of one or more of the "big five." Mike Cannon, then the clerk of court for East Baton Rouge Parish, was adept at involving these groups and even helped create a couple of them. I wanted to have them in my corner from the start. To make sure that they were in and wouldn't go a different way, I set out to meet with their leaders early in my campaign.

I called Joe Delpit, a supporter of mine from the start. My relationship with him began in 1966, when I was a job developer with the South Baton Rouge Employment Agency, located on East Boulevard and Washington Street. Joe was just starting to get involved in community and neighborhood issues and politics through the South Baton Rouge (SBR) Advisory Council. The Advisory Council did just that, overseeing the Neighborhood Service Center's operations and acting as a quasi-board of directors. When he was a member of the Baton Rouge City Council, Joe recruited me to take on the position of federal aid coordinator.

The Chicken Shack, a Delpit family business located on Lettsworth Street just a couple of blocks from the Service Center, was a popular place for good soul food and the locus of social and political action activities. Candidates running for political office invariably would find their way to "the Shack" to get Joe's endorsement and ostensibly that of the South Baton Rouge Advisory Council. Joe told me how Senator Russell Long had stopped by the Chicken Shack to solicit his support and found him working in the kitchen making potato salad. The senator asked for some and enjoyed a meal of fried chicken and potato salad while making his pitch for an endorsement. It wasn't unusual to find elected officials and political wannabes there. The Chicken Shack was indeed the intersection of soul food and politics in South Baton Rouge.

I explained the demographic situation and how we could overcome it with a massive turnout. In order to do so, we had to put together a strong campaign team, starting with naming a campaign manager. I had several individuals in mind but didn't want to make any overtures until I talked to Joe. He thought I should get somebody with a relatively high profile, who was in good standing in the Black community, and had credibility in the white community. Such an individual would give me credibility with those who didn't know me but were familiar with the campaign manager.

While discussing the potential candidates for campaign manager, Press Robinson's name popped up. Press was the first Black elected to the East Baton Rouge School Board. He held a Ph.D. in chemistry and was a tenured faculty member at Southern University. Folks often commented about how well-spoken Press was. I didn't know him well enough to make a cold call for such a big ask. Joe told me the key to Press was Dick Turnley.

Turnley was the first Black elected to the State House of Representatives from Baton Rouge in modern times. His legislative district covered Scotlandville and North Baton Rouge. Turnley, Press, and Councilman Jewel Newman were the power brokers behind the Scotlandville Advisory Committee (SAC). I needed them to play a significant role in my campaign. Joe called Turnley and told him he was helping me put together a campaign for city court and thought that Press would be the ideal person to serve as my campaign manager. Turnley replied, "You know, that could work. Press's reelection is coming up soon, and the extra visibility might also work to his benefit." Joe hung up the phone and said, "Now we can call Press. He will not say yes right away because he'll want to run it by Dick." I made the call, and the scenario worked out just as Joe suggested. Press called me back and said he would accept the role of campaign manager. His advice throughout the campaign proved invaluable.

I contacted my old high school football coach, George E. Mencer, who had left coaching to become a school principal, and asked him to serve as my campaign treasurer. We enlisted the help of Mr. John Vaughn, a retired business executive who had moved back to Baton Rouge from Chicago, to help him. Both Coach Mencer and Mr. Vaughn were highly respected and well regarded throughout Black and white communities. Getting them on board gave my campaign credibility with an older generation.

Delpit suggested it would be wise to get Louis Jetson and the Gus Young Civic Association on board early. Their support would likely pique the interest of State Representative Kevin Reilly, a close ally of Jetson, and possibly get some help from Lamar Advertising, Representative Reilly's family business. Later in the campaign, I met with Representative Reilly, and he donated eight billboards to my campaign for city court judge. The billboards were strategically located in and around Black neighborhoods, which gave my campaign ready visibility. His caveat was that I had to pay for the paper that the artwork would appear on, though all the rental and labor costs would be free.

Joe also mentioned Acie Belton. I told him that I knew Mr. Belton through my father, as both had worked together at what is now Exxon for years. I felt that he would support my efforts.

I happened to run into Art Smith, a white attorney I had met years ago while attending political meetings sponsored by the Capital City Democratic Association (CCDA). He was heavily involved in Democratic politics through CCDA. He mentioned he had heard I was running for Baton Rouge City Court and wanted to know if there was anything he could do to help. I told him I needed to map out a strategy for engaging white voters. He referred me to someone who had worked in Dutch Morial's mayoral campaign in New Orleans.

Ernest "Dutch" Morial had won a historic victory to become mayor of New Orleans. Citywide demographics were not on his side. Nonetheless, he consolidated all the Black political groups (such as SOUL, BOLD, LIFE, and COUP) and won enough of the white vote to claim victory. Since I was also running citywide, I was sure there were lessons to be learned from Morial's campaign.

Art and I drove down to New Orleans to meet with David Marcello, the young white attorney he had spoken of earlier. Michael Bagneris, a young African American lawyer who had also worked in the Morial campaign, joined us in the meeting. Michael later won a race for a judgeship on the Orleans Civil District Court.

It became apparent that we had to run a well-organized and targeted campaign in the white community simultaneously with our robust campaign targeting Black voters. Hence, it was imperative to form a separate committee and find a separate individual to manage my outreach to the white community. The key was to have two different campaign committees (one Black, one white) coordinating their efforts to ensure the messages from me to the two communities were not contradictory. Fundraising was also critical and was tasked to the separate committees.

In contemplating making a run for office, I stopped by the headquarters of the Louisiana Association of Business and Industry (LABI) to get copies of several pamphlets they published about organizing and running political campaigns. LABI's membership, primarily Republican leaning, would not likely endorse a Democrat like me, nor would the group likely be interested in helping my campaign. Nonetheless, their literature was excellent, and I found it quite helpful.

One of LABI's pamphlets described the makeup of a viable campaign team. Not only did it describe each of the team positions, but it also outlined their duties and responsibilities. I knew I needed a campaign manager and treasurer, but I knew nothing about having a volunteer coordinator, a public relations coordinator, and an events scheduler. Another LABI pamphlet explained how to set up a phone bank and develop its messaging. I was eager to get my campaign team in place.

In keeping with David Marcello's advice, I needed to name a co-campaign manager who could help me focus on the white community. I immediately thought of Charles "Chick" Moore, a highly respected trial lawyer, Baton Rouge Bar and Louisiana Trial Lawyers Association member, and a good friend. Chick and I had met several years earlier as opposing counsel in the *State of Louisiana v. Walter Monroe*. I was an assistant district attorney in the East Baton Rouge District Attorney's Office at the time, assigned to prosecuting Walter Monroe for second-degree murder. Chick was his defense attorney. I inherited the case two months before the trial date after I had complained to my section chief, Lennie Perez, that I didn't join the DA's Office to be stuck trying misdemeanors. Lennie gave me the *State of Louisiana v. Walter Monroe* case to try.

I should have sensed that something was off with the case, but my zeal to become a top prosecutor clouded my view. It was a jury trial; that's what I had asked for, and that's what I got. I immediately dug into the file, noticing that the defendant had entered a dual plea of "not guilty" and "not guilty by reason of insanity." It was the defendant's burden to prove that he didn't know right from wrong when entering such a plea. The sanity commission that the judge appointed found Walter Monroe sane and capable of assisting counsel in his defense. My burden, as the prosecutor, was to prove that the defendant committed every element of the crime of second-degree murder while also demonstrating that he indeed knew right from wrong, thus negating his insanity defense. I had a short time in which to absorb a lot of information. This case would be my first jury trial as a lawyer.

The murder itself occurred just as the defendant and his girlfriend drove into East Baton Rouge Parish. Monroe was behind the wheel. The victim was in the passenger seat. In the backseat were two acquaintances who were boyfriend and girlfriend. They testified that as Monroe drove along chatting pleasantly, he suddenly raised a pistol and calmly shot his girlfriend in the head. After shooting her, he kept driving and continued to talk with them as if nothing had happened. They were horrified and feared he would turn around and shoot them too, but he just kept driving through Baton Rouge and over the bridge into West Baton Rouge. When the defendant finally stopped at a red light, they bolted from the car.

Though this was my first jury trial, I thought I was well prepared. I did everything right, asked all the right questions, laid the proper foundation to get in evidence, and made all of the correct objections. As the trial progressed, however, I felt I was losing the jury. Chick Moore did an excellent job setting them up to find his client not guilty and not guilty by reason of insanity. His expert witness, a psychiatrist, handily contradicted the sanity commission members' testimony.

Moreover, the defendant acted up in the courtroom in such a way that it seemed he was, in fact, insane. I couldn't blame the jury when it returned verdicts of not guilty and not guilty by reason of insanity. From the prosecution's standpoint, these verdicts were not a complete loss. The defendant was taken into custody and committed to a mental institution, where he would remain until he was no longer deemed a threat or danger to himself or society.

Chick was excited to join my campaign and was all in, and his law partner Ed Walters came aboard too and agreed to take on the role of assistant campaign treasurer. Lennie Perez, my old section chief from the District Attorney's Office; Mike Patterson; John Noland; and Lewis Unglesby were just a few of the white attorneys who supported me early on. David Roach was my professional political consultant, and Leroy Kolter was my public relations consultant. They served as my campaign team's core and helped develop my messaging to the white community.

I also needed support from the predominantly white Baton Rouge Bar Association. It was a plus that I was formerly an assistant district attorney and enjoyed an excellent reputation with the local legal community.

Chick drafted a letter to the Baton Rouge Bar Association members asking them to join the committee to elect me judge of the Baton Rouge City Court. The letter got a great response, and the committee jumped from ten members to twenty-five and then to more than one hundred. Chick's letter also encouraged committee members to reach out to their clients on my behalf. Our next goal was to place a full-page advertisement in both the *Morning Advocate* and *State-Times* newspapers listing all of the lawyers who endorsed me. In all, nearly one hundred attorneys did so. The ads ran on March 24, 1983, two days before the election. In the final analysis, more than 250 lawyers had joined my campaign committee.

As the Christmas holidays set in, I began to attend numerous holiday parties, pass out push cards, and promote my candidacy. Supporters started stopping by our office to offer their assistance. Carolyn Ricks and Monica O'Connor, our secretaries, were too busy handling the work of the five attorneys in the office to deal with the steady stream of people stopping by to offer help with my campaign. It became necessary for me to hire a part-time person to handle and coordinate the campaign volunteer efforts. I still had a full-time law practice. My clients expected me to handle their needs in a prompt, efficient, and professional manner. Mazie Roberson, the wife of attorney Lon Roberson, became my campaign scheduler. I told her I needed help with my campaign speech schedule and tasked her with finding meetings and events around town to promote my candidacy for city court judge. Wherever there was a gathering of people, large or small, I wanted to be there. I suggested that she introduce herself to Mayor Pat Screen's secretary, who could advise her about all of the mayor's open events to which I could show up and pass out my campaign push cards.

I also solicited Rosemary Alexander's help. She was on leave from her job as a flight attendant. Rosemary helped organize campaign operations, which included setting up a telephone bank. Our law office had two telephone lines, and I had three additional lines installed to have five in-house lines for our phone bank. Volunteers also made calls from their homes.

With election day drawing near, it was about time to make sure our get-out-the-vote (GOTV) plans were in place. Representative Delpit offered to coordinate our GOTV efforts on election day. I stopped by the Chicken

Shack to update him on what was going on at headquarters. Joe assured me that everything was under control and that a meeting had already been called for the heads of all the local Black organizations to meet at the Chicken Shack to discuss GOTV activities. Though I could not make it to the meeting, Press Robinson, my campaign manager, represented me.

Fifteen political organizations attended, and all agreed to endorse me and sign off on a single ballot to be distributed citywide before and on the day of the election. Such a show of support was absolutely unprecedented. Even more astounding was their decision not to assess my campaign any cost for their endorsements, assistance, or support. Such an assessment could have run into the thousands of dollars, given the number of canvassers each organization would provide on election day. I was overwhelmed and asked Joe how he got everyone on board. He told me they all knew my longtime community involvement and reputation as a lawyer and felt supporting my candidacy was the right thing to do. My election would make history, and they all wanted to be a part of it.

Even though we didn't have to deal with costs associated with getting out the vote, the expense of running a campaign was mounting fast. Every group needed voter lists for the precincts for which they were responsible, along with corresponding telephone numbers. We had to have copies at the campaign headquarters to back up all of the GOTV operations. I turned to Chick Moore, Lennie Perez, and John Noland to make some fundraising calls. I also asked Genevieve Stewart, a local talk show host, my neighbor and friend, and the wife of Dr. Luther Stewart, to help organize a fundraising event. Genevieve agreed and coordinated a fundraiser she dubbed a "Champagne Sip," which was held at a local banquet facility. This fundraiser's goal was twofold, to raise money and generate a lot of excitement and enthusiasm. That meant the tickets had to be affordable. We settled upon the price of twenty-five dollars per ticket. Genevieve and Harriet pulled together a group of ladies to serve as hostesses. They decorated the facility as if it was a much pricier event.

A good friend from my old neighborhood, Leroy Pero, and his band of outstanding musicians provided the music for free. All of the champagne was donated. The catering facility provided finger food and a cash bar if guests desired something besides champagne. All of the political organizations that endorsed me received at least five tickets to the event. My campaign manager presented a short endorsement speech, followed by State Representative Joe Delpit and Senator Richard Turnley. I gave a brief but fiery address to the large crowd. Borrowing from Victor Hugo, I said, "There is no force more powerful than an idea whose time has come, and on March 26, 1983, Baton Rouge will elect a Black man to a seat on the Baton Rouge City Court, and that Black man will be me."

Initially, we questioned whether we could make money after expenses, but we did. We collected a sizable sum, as more than four hundred people attended the event that night. Quite a few lawyers came and brought checks far exceeding the twenty-five-dollar price of the ticket. Thankfully, we accomplished both of our objectives for this event. People were both generous and excited by my prospects.

### On Integrating the Judiciary in Louisiana

African Americans' political fortunes began to take shape with the 1964 Civil Rights Act and the 1965 Voting Rights Act. In Baton Rouge and other southern cities, African Americans began to take seats on city and parish (county) governing boards, and several were elected to state legislatures. However, what was quite clear was that the judicial leg of the three-legged stool of government was not as readily accessible to the African American lawyers vying for judgeships. The door cracked open in Louisiana when Governor John J. McKeithen appointed Israel Augustine Jr. to an Orleans Parish Criminal District Court judgeship in 1969.

Governor McKeithen had two candidates in mind to fill a vacancy on the Orleans Parish Criminal District Court: Israel Augustine Jr. and Ernest "Dutch" Morial, the first African American elected to the Louisiana House of Representatives since Reconstruction and a supporter of the governor's legislative initiatives. Rumor had it that Governor Mc-Keithen was impressed with Augustine's efforts to calm the 1969 student uprising at Southern University in New Orleans. After much deliberation, he got the seat, becoming the first Black judge to serve in Louisiana since Reconstruction.

In 1971, Augustine ran for and became the first elected Black judge in Louisiana, winning the same seat on the Orleans Criminal District Court. He presided over the Black Panther trial that year, which brought him national attention and helped him win a seat on the Louisiana Fourth Circuit Court of Appeal in 1981. Although Morial did not get Governor McKeithen's initial appointment to the bench, he was appointed to a seat on the Orleans Parish Juvenile Court in 1971. Morial added another pioneering accomplishment with his election to the Fourth Circuit Court of Appeals one year later. Governor Edwin Edwards, like Governor McKeithen, took notice of the changing demographics of New Orleans and realized there was political capital in appointing an African American to the bench. Therefore, he appointed Joan Bernard Armstrong to the Orleans Parish Juvenile Court, filling the vacancy left by Ernest Morial. That appointment gave Armstrong a sense of incumbency, which helped her attract enough white voters to win the seat when it came up for election.

Judicial appointments by Louisiana governors occurred until the ratification of the 1974 Louisiana Constitution. The new constitution eliminated the governor's power to appoint, giving the Louisiana Supreme Court that power instead. If one was lucky enough to be appointed by the state supreme court, the constitution prohibited them from running for the position after their appointment expired.

Revius Ortique Jr., a prominent attorney in New Orleans, was the first Black appointed to the bench under the new rules set out in the constitution. The Louisiana Supreme Court appointed him to the Orleans Civil District Court in 1974. He was appointed to complete a departing judge's unexpired term, with the understanding that he wouldn't be able to run for that seat. However, before the term expired, another division of the court opened. Ortique campaigned for that second opening while still serving as a judge ad hoc on the Orleans Civil District Court. To many, he was running as an incumbent, which contributed significantly to his election win.

Interestingly, my research showed that no African American politician appeared at any constitutional convention hearings to voice opposition to the drastic change in the rules of judicial appointment. But there was a plethora of evidence that African Americans were heavily involved in all other aspects of the convention. It became apparent that African American politicians didn't perceive the importance of having Black lawyers appointed and subsequently elected to Louisiana's judgeships. Moreover, it seemed that Governor Edwards didn't mind giving up his power to appoint attorneys to fill vacant judicial seats.

## Getting the Newspapers' Endorsement

The *Morning Advocate* and *State-Times* newspapers routinely interviewed all judicial candidates and then endorsed one. The day they asked to interview me conflicted with the jury trial I had on my schedule. In past years judicial candidates were granted continuances if they had such a conflict. My motion for a continuance was summarily denied. I asked the judge, with whom I had good relations, for reconsideration and was again denied. However, I did get him to concede to an extended recess, giving me time to go to my interview.

Defending a client accused of simple burglary in a jury trial and then composing myself to cogently and sufficiently answer questions from an editorial board was somewhat daunting. I needed to focus on picking a jury and defending my client rather than on impressing newspaper staffers. The trial started. We recessed for the interview as planned. I fielded all of the reporters' questions and thought I gave credible responses. It would be a couple of weeks before I found out the editorial board's decision.

After my interview, I returned to court to resume the trial, which lasted two days due to the recess. The jury returned a verdict of "not guilty" for my client. After the proceedings, the judge called me up to the bench and told me I could have waived the jury and tried the case before him. He said he would have likewise found my client not guilty. That tack would have freed me up for my interview with the editorial board. I believe the judge realized he had put me in a tough position and tried to smooth it over.

On March 23, I received the endorsement of both newspapers. The first endorsement read: "After interviewing both [candidates] and studying their backgrounds, the Morning Advocate is recommending a vote for Freddie 'Fred' Pitcher, Jr. . . . . The Advocate feels that he would make a better city judge for Baton Rouge."

The *State-Times* endorsement stated, "Following the interview of both candidates, . . . it is the consensus of the editorial board of this newspaper that Pitcher is the better candidate."

Though neither endorsement was overly glowing, both papers chose to endorse a Black candidate over a white candidate. This was unprecedented, and I hoped it would sway some white voters my way.

I thought the last paragraph of the *State-Times* endorsement went a long way toward taking race out of the electoral equation with the statement that "Mr. Pitcher is black and Mr. Weatherford is white. This difference has been of no consequence in previous public legal service by these two candidates, and we would urge that it not influence your choice in Saturday's special election."

## Countdown to Election Day

Part of our campaign strategy was to jump-start our phone bank three days prior to the March 26 election. We had an extensive list of volunteers to draw from, the core of whom were Harriet's professional colleagues and former students, our cousins, friends, church members, and many of my high school classmates.

Up to the day before the election, we had achieved all of the goals we had set out to accomplish. We had solicited and galvanized both the Black church community and Black political organizations. We made at least two phone calls to each voter on our constituent list and sent out several thousand mailers resembling telegrams, which targeted Black female voters. Our research had shown that they were the most likely voters to go to the polls. I had walked neighborhoods, visited beauty parlors and barbershops, and stood in front of grocery stores handing out push cards. On Sundays, I spoke at practically every Black church in the city. Our campaign outreach was broad and wide-ranging in the Black community, while our outreach to the white community was more targeted and lower key. We were looking to maximize Black voter turnout and pick up at least 15 percent of the white vote. A few of my white friends invited me to speak at small gatherings at their homes, which led to more invitations to speak, resulting in "Freddie Pitcher for City Judge" signs springing up in white neighborhoods throughout the city.

The remaining question on the eve of election day was whether or not we had done enough.

Our efforts to increase the number of attorneys to join our campaign got a lot of traction, rising to more than one hundred, some of whom signed onto a full-page advertisement published in both newspapers on March 24, two days before the election.

## Election Day

On March 26, 1983, we awakened to the roar of thunder, lightning flashing, and a heavy downpour of rain. Suddenly I had a hollow feeling that the storm would undercut all of our planning and hard work. The adage that Black folks don't go out to vote in the rain began to haunt me. I could only hope and pray that the weather would subside and we could inspire our voters to head to the polls.

We began the morning with a prayer breakfast at Belfair Baptist Church, where Harriet, Kyla, and I were members, and where I served on the deacon board. Our pastor, Rev. Alvin A. Francois, led off with a prayer of thanksgiving and deliverance, followed by Deacon John James, a longtime family friend and godparent to Kyla, who delivered another moving and powerful prayer for victory. Despite the rain, the breakfast was well attended by our church members and our campaign staff.

Harriet and I left the prayer breakfast and headed to our polling place, just around the corner from our house in Concord Estates. After voting, I dropped my wife and daughter off at home and headed to the campaign headquarters in my law office. I was anxious to see how the rain was impacting turnout. Supporters in our targeted precincts were going to the polls despite the weather. Reports from our political groups indicated they were buying umbrellas and raincoats anywhere they could to help voters get to the polls. When umbrellas were not available, they resorted to using big plastic bags to protect folks from the rain. It kept raining, but people kept defying the adage that Black folks don't go out to vote in the rain!

We planned to have poll watchers in all Black precincts who would feed voter turnout information back to headquarters. Precinct canvassers knocked on the doors of those who had not yet voted and encouraged them to do so. We also had poll watchers in key predominantly white precincts to help us gauge if we were meeting our 15 percent turnout goal. Our expectation from the outset was that we would outperform the voter turnout in the white community percentage-wise. Having poll watchers in key white precincts enabled us to assess the strength of turnout for Bill Weatherford.

As the inclement weather began to break, early reports indicated that turnout in the Black areas was higher than white turnout. I sensed that something extraordinary was about to happen. All we needed was to make sure that we didn't lighten up on our push for voter turnout. The election was about more than me. The Black community in Baton Rouge was on the verge of claiming full inclusion in the city's political process. It appeared I would be the instrument through which that was to happen.

The sun came out around noon, and the remainder of the day was gorgeous. From all indications, our GOTV operations were working well. Our campaign had drivers taking people to the polls. We had volunteers calling voters who had yet to vote. Louis Hamilton and I crisscrossed the city, driving from precinct to precinct, trying to assess the turnout. Campaign headquarters was bustling with activity. Ralph Tyson, Don Avery, Tim Hardy, Edselle Cunningham, and Elaine Boyle filled in wherever needed. My brother Larry and several of his friends, Clyde Brandon, Jackie Ray Brown, and Gilbert Wilson, worked tirelessly to get our signs all over the city. They were also providing transportation and driving voters to the polls.

As reports trickled in, it appeared something was amiss at the designated polling place for the avenues behind Southern University. Turnout was sparse, and we needed to find out the cause. After talking to several people in the area, we learned that many of the residents were unaware that their neighborhood's recent annexation into the city limits allowed them to vote in this particular election for city court judge. We quickly organized a large caravan of cars and trucks led by Rev. Don Avery. They sounded off air horns, blew car horns, and knocked on doors to let the residents know that they could vote in this election and that they should vote for Freddie Pitcher. According to the poll watcher we assigned to that precinct, our tactic worked because people there were still in line to vote at poll closing.

As the Big Bertha precincts started to report into the night, we began to catch up and surge ahead after languishing behind for most of the evening and remained in the lead until the polls closed. We were ecstatic! We had prevailed despite demographics that were not in our favor. We proved the naysayers wrong.

I received 16,581 votes, representing 57 percent of the total votes cast to Bill Weatherford's 12,717 votes, representing 43 percent of the votes. It was a historic victory!

Sunday morning, the day after the election, Harriet, Kyla, and I got up early, dressed, and headed off to church. We wanted to start the new day by giving thanks to the Almighty for the beautiful blessing bestowed upon me and my family. Before we left, the front doorbell rang. Television and newspaper reporters were at our door asking for a statement on how I felt about my historic victory. I repeated what I had said the previous evening, which was that I was elated and looking forward to getting right to work as a judge on the Baton Rouge City Court. One reporter asked if I thought it was way past time to elect a Black judge. Not wanting to give them something that might create a sensational headline, I just said, "I will not speak to the then, only to the now, and yesterday and now are my time."

Services had already begun by the time we arrived at church. As we entered, the congregation erupted in applause. Pastor Francois invited us to come up to the front. He altered the order of service and began to recount my electoral victory. I couldn't stop the tears from welling up in my eyes over what had happened. When asked to speak, all I could do was thank God, the Belfair Church family, and our friends and supporters. My election was a victory not only for me and my family but also a victory for all of the Black citizens of Baton Rouge.

Over the next several days, we began planning for my investiture ceremony in coordination with the Baton Rouge Bar Association. I wanted to recognize as many supporters as I could by including them in the investiture program. A touchy situation arose when someone suggested that Dr. T. J. Jemison deliver the invocation. I had initially planned to ask Rev. Ulysses Hayes to provide the invocation to show my gratitude for all he had done. Reverend Hayes worked tirelessly throughout the entire campaign, arranging for all of my Sunday church visits. He had scheduled me to visit three or four churches each Sunday. Every Friday he brought me the list of churches to attend that weekend, arranging everything with the pastors beforehand. Those pushing for Dr. Jemison to give the invocation emphasized his position as the president of the National Baptist Association, U.S.A., Inc., citing protocol and tradition in the Baptist Church. I gave in and asked Reverend Hayes to deliver the benediction; I could tell that he was disappointed that Jemison was providing the invocation. I reminded him that his position on the program would give him the last word, and having the last word meant that he had the opportunity to put the final touch on our making history in Baton Rouge. That seemed to improve his disposition, and he agreed to give the benediction.

On the morning of my swearing-in ceremony, Harriet, Kyla, and I made our way downtown to the Municipal Building and proceeded to the Old Council Chambers for the ceremony. We went to an adjacent room where the Baton Rouge City Court judges had assembled with Mickey Skyring, the clerk of court for city court. As I anxiously waited for the ceremony to start, Byron Stringer said, "Freddie, I hope you can be stronger than I was at my investiture; I had an outpouring of emotions and cried when I tried to speak." I said, "I think I can hold it." When we finally marched into the Council Chambers, thunderous applause greeted us. My emotions did get the better of me. Tears welled up in my eyes and began to flow down my cheeks.

The day of my investiture was a historic day for me, my family, and the entire African American community in East Baton Rouge Parish.

### Elected Judge: Baton Rouge City Court

The Baton Rouge City Court, which I worked so hard to join, is a court of limited jurisdiction. It has civil jurisdiction over lawsuits of up to fifteen thousand dollars and criminal jurisdiction over misdemeanor offenses, in which the maximum jail sentences cannot exceed six months and fines cannot exceed five hundred dollars. City court is considered the people's court and is the first and only court experience most people will have with the judicial system throughout their entire lives. Most litigant exposure involves contesting a traffic ticket, filing or defending against a small-claim lawsuit, or defending against a misdemeanor criminal matter. Such experiences shape the average person's perception of the entire judicial system. The temperament of the judge plays a vital role in shaping that perception.

As a young lawyer representing clients in courtrooms in and around Baton Rouge, I witnessed numerous occasions where white judges were discourteous to the Black litigants who appeared before them. Disparaging someone just because one has the power to do so is wrong, and wearing a judicial robe doesn't make it right. That was not the kind of judge I wanted to be. Treating everyone with dignity and respect was central to how I wanted to operate. Listening, being patient, and hearing litigants out was how I wanted to run my court. Nonetheless, occasionally I had to raise my voice to get someone's attention or to maintain decorum in the courtroom.

The novelty of a Black judge was baffling to many of the Black litigants who appeared before me. They would often address me as Mr. Pitcher while using the title Judge when referring to my white counterparts. After getting past being upset, I realized they were not being intentionally disrespectful. Seeing a Black man in a robe was something new for them, and it was my job to educate them that I was to be called Judge Pitcher. Four years later, when Black judges Tyson and Calloway got elected, they experienced the same thing. Having a Black judge dispense justice in Baton Rouge was a novel phenomenon for both litigants and attorneys. On several occasions, I had to remind unruly lawyers who presided over the courtroom.

What I didn't anticipate having was a problem with any of the local police officers. When I was an assistant district attorney, many of them served as witnesses in cases I prosecuted in district court. Several of the criminal cases I handled were high-profile, which required that I work very closely with police officers, especially those in the detective division. Although I expected to encounter some displeasure with me being Black and making decisions affecting white people, I never expected a police officer to have the gall to come right out and voice his displeasure with me as a judge and question how I exercised my authority in that position.

Early in my tenure on the bench, I encountered a police officer who epitomized the racist undercurrent in the force. I distinctly recall having just started my rotation as the duty judge at noon on a Friday when I received a call from an old high school acquaintance, "Skinny" Pearson, the brother of my former homeroom classmate Roger Pearson.

I knew Skinny to be an upstanding person and gainfully employed. He asked me if he could serve as personal surety and sign the bond for his nephew, who had been arrested on a traffic bench warrant. I told him I'd call the booking desk and authorize him to sign his nephew out on a personal surety bond.

Shortly after that, I learned that Skinny was being jailed on an old bench warrant for a traffic ticket. I called to inquire about the situation, after which I instructed officers on the booking desk to let Mr. Pearson sign himself out and give him notice to appear in my court on Monday morning. When asked about his nephew, I told them to let him sign his nephew out as well and give them both notices to appear in my court on Monday morning.

That evening my wife and I were preparing to attend the Omega Psi Phi fraternity's annual gala when I received another telephone call from the booking desk. The caller informed me that an article in the morning paper would describe how my bond-setting policy put the people of Baton Rouge at risk by letting criminals back out on the street after they had been arrested. He characterized my bond-setting policy to the paper as a revolving door. The caller then informed me that he was the one who provided the information to the press and emphasized that he wanted me to know it was him.

His tone of voice was quite belligerent and clearly intended to intimidate or scare me. Trying to stay calm, I told him that I didn't view traffic offenders as hardened criminals who must sit in jail over the weekend when accommodations can be made through the bonding process to get them to return and take care of their business with the court.

I was now outraged and felt the need to strike back. After I calmed down, I called Chief of Police Wayne Rogillio and apprised him of what had just happened. He also became incensed and told me he would take care of it. Harriet and I went to the gala, but the unexpected turn of events essentially ruined our evening.

The Saturday morning newspaper carried an article portraying my policy on setting bonds as "a revolving door," attributing the information to local police officers. Ironically, another piece printed several pages further into the same newspaper described me as a tough-on-crime judge.

The officer's action got him suspended for several days and confined to the police station's bowels as a radio room operator, a punishment most officers dreaded.

When I arrived at the courthouse on Monday, police officers who were usually very cordial to me were suddenly less welcoming. "I guess you guys read the story in the newspaper," I said. "The source of the story will soon be transferred over to Wooddale Boulevard. You know what's on Wooddale, don't you?" The reply was "No!" I said, "the unemployment office," in a somewhat joking manner.

As a result of my passing comment to the few officers sitting around on that Monday morning, an onslaught of letters to the editor by alleged concerned citizens suddenly appeared, implying that I was using my power as a judge to get a dedicated police officer fired. Hardly a week went by without at least one letter appearing on the newspaper editorial page, attacking me as a vindictive judge. No reporter asked me for my side of the story to ascertain why the police chief took the punitive actions he did against the officer.

I did not know the officer in question before my encounter with him that Friday, but I soon learned he was serving his second stint on the Baton Rouge city police force. His first stint ended when he joined a group of officers protesting the new policy pairing Black and white officers as riding partners in police units. The protesters walked into the chief of police's office, tossed their badges on his desk, and quit the force in a flagrant demonstration of racial prejudice and discrimination. Any one of them allowed to return to the force, in my estimation, made a mockery of a police department that allegedly professed to be against racial bias and discrimination. This officer didn't want to ride with Black officers back then, and now he did not want to take orders from a Black judge.

After I was bombarded with letters to the editor for several weeks, fellow judge Byron Stringer suggested that I give the editor of the *State-Times* a call and ask for a meeting. I followed his advice and scheduled a date and time to meet with the editorial board of both newspapers. I told them that I wanted to let them know what happened between the officer and me and relate to them how the officer in question had called me and tried to intimidate me into letting people languish in jail over minor offenses.

I asked how the press could publish an article saying I was putting the people of Baton Rouge at risk because of my bonding policy, and then, several pages later, in the same paper, carry an article touting my toughness as a judge. The room fell quiet. I was then asked to step out of the room for a few minutes, which I did.

I was invited back in and told that no more letters to the editor attacking me on this issue would be printed. They also invited me to write a letter they would publish in response to all the letters written against me. I informed them that I was not interested in doing so. My goal was to apprise them of what had happened and suggest that if these defaming letters continued, the newspaper would be complicit in attacking the first and only Black judge in this city. One of the associate editors responded by saying that the papers knew that this same officer had thrown his badge on the police chief's desk several years ago and resigned from the force.

I questioned why they gave his supporters such a platform to denigrate me, but they offered no response. However, no more letters to the editor were published, ending a very stressful period in the early days of my judgeship on Baton Rouge City Court.

One of the things I enjoyed doing was speaking to students at schools throughout the parish on topics ranging from what it was like to be a judge to the perils of getting caught up in the criminal justice system. I was particularly interested in speaking invitations from predominantly Black schools. As the first and only Black judge in Baton Rouge, I knew that I had a duty to serve as a role model, and I relished the task. It kept me on the run, but I felt it was my obligation. In addition to speaking to individual classes at the invitation of their teachers, I also participated in the local Adopt-a-School Program. The program encouraged the business community and other groups to partner with schools in and around the parish to help with needs not budgeted by the school system. An elaborate ceremony that mirrored a judicial adoption was put in place for students to witness. Such school adoption events were often the first time Black students got to see a real Black judge. Many of them initially assumed I was a preacher because of the black robe I wore. Judge Frank Polozola of the Federal Middle District Court of Louisiana and I traveled the Adopt-a-School circuit together. We received special recognition from the East Baton Rouge School Board for our participation in the program.

Because of all of the preelection campaigning I had done in Black churches, I remained on their speakers' circuit. I felt that I had a duty and responsibility to give back to the people who overwhelmingly supported me and helped me make history. So, when called upon to speak, I readily responded.

Aerial photo of Valley Park, taken in 1954. The landfill
of the old dump is at center right.

Watercolor drawing depicting Owens Grocery and neighborhood boys.
Drawing by Samuel Cobb.

In the army. At left I'm shown at my station in
Baumholder, Germany, in 1968.

Southern University's Law Week in 1971–72. S. P. Davis, Barry Edwards,
and I received Outstanding Moot Court Competition recognition
from Professors Thomas Brown and Louis Berry.

Pictured with Georgia state senator and civil rights activist Julian Bond on the night of my election to the Baton Rouge City Court.

Seated with my wife and daughter, next to Rev. Ulas Hayes and Dr. T. J. Jemison, at the City Court investiture ceremony.

Co-campaign manager Charles Moore, with Robert Leake, Tim Hardy,
Ralph Tyson, Don Avery, and other supporters
at the City Court investiture.

Here I take the oath of office with Judge Israel Augustine Jr.
as my daughter Kyla holds the Bible.

Attorney Charles Moore presents me with my first judicial robe
as my wife Harriet looks on.

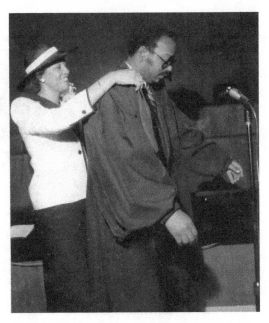

Being robed by wife Harriet after taking my
oath of office as a judge on the
Baton Rouge City Court.

Seated enbanc with Judges Byron Stringer, Rosemary Pillow, and Darrell White.

Being congratulated by Councilman Joseph Delpit.

My wife and I pose with campaign manager Dr. Press
Robinson and Mrs. Robinson at the reception
following the swearing-in ceremony.

At the reception with my mother, Mrs. Lucy Pitcher; my
sister, Juanita Winfield; and my brothers Floyd and Larry.

Family seated at my district court investiture. *Left to right*: My brother Glynn Pitcher, sister-in-law Janice Pitcher, brothers Larry and Floyd, father Freddie Sr., mother Lucy, brother-in-law Russell Winfield, and sister Juanita.

Being sworn in as a judge on the Louisiana First Circuit Court of Appeal by Circuit Judge Melvin Shortess while my wife and daughter look on.

En banc photo of the Louisiana First Circuit Court of
Appeal during my time on it.

Several faculty members from the Southern University Law Center
presented papers at the University of Lagos in 1995 as part of the
Democracy in Africa program. Standing with me in the foreground
are ambassador to Nigeria Walter C. Carrington, Bishop
Desmond Tutu, and Professor Russell Jones. Behind us are
Professor Akintunde O. Obilade, Dr. Gloria Braxton,
and Professor Jacqueline Nash.

While in Nigeria, Dr. Braxton and I were made honorary chiefs of
the township of Idoko in Osun State. Here we pose with
the oba and other village leaders.

Visiting with Mrs. Inez Chrisentery, my sixth-grade teacher, at a
reception for my retirement from the Court of Appeal.

In my chancellor's robes. Both my daughter Kyla and my wife Harriet
bear the title "Dr.," having earned advanced degrees in
musical arts and education, respectively.

Standing in front of Owens Grocery in 2022.

# 5

## Making Another Run

### *Nineteenth Judicial District Court*

**A**FTER SERVING AS a judge on the Baton Rouge City Court for four and a half years, I began to consider running for the district court. I had already presided over several hundred civil, criminal, and traffic trials, sentenced people to jail, and placed a few hundred folks on probation for various misdemeanor offenses. During my 1983 run for the city court I promised to serve out the five and a half years left on the term if elected. I discussed moving up to the district court with the other three judges on my court: Rosemary Pillow, Byron Stringer, and Darrell White. They were all content to remain on the city court bench.

In September of 1984, after serving only a little over a year on the city court bench, the Louisiana Supreme Court appointed me as a district judge ad hoc in the Nineteenth Judicial District. It was a one-month appointment to replace Judge John Covington upon his election to the Louisiana First Circuit Court of Appeal. I saw this appointment as an excellent opportunity to demonstrate that I was up to the task of being a district court judge. During that one-month ad hoc appointment, I handled everything on my docket, including preliminary hearings, motions to suppress, misdemeanor trials, and even a jury trial. Short-term ad hoc judge appointments often resulted in many matters on the docket being continued for the newly elected judge to handle. I chose to clear as many cases as possible to demonstrate that I could handle any issue a district judge would routinely address. As with my appointment to the city court, I believed this ad hoc appointment would benefit me in a future run for the district court.

While handling my docket one morning, I noticed attorneys Janice Clark and Murphy Bell sitting together in the courtroom, even though neither one had a matter before me. I assumed they were there to see me about something other than the misdemeanor trials scheduled for that day, so I took a recess and asked them to approach the bench. In a sidebar, Murphy Bell, the more senior of the two, told me that they were about to file a suit to challenge the racial composition of the courts in East Baton Rouge Parish, including the Baton Rouge City Court, and wanted to give me the courtesy of a heads-up. Janice was somewhat ambivalent about including city court in the lawsuit. She wanted the suit to be statewide and aimed at general jurisdiction courts, not city or municipal courts. Murphy felt differently.

I told them I had no problem with it, but that including the Baton Rouge City Court might prove problematic. The opposition would use my successful run to counter their contention that Blacks cannot get elected under the current at-large system of electing judges. I knew that Louis A. Martinet Society members had been meeting and considering filing a lawsuit to dismantle the at-large method of electing judges in East Baton Rouge Parish. As a sitting judge, I could not be involved in those meetings, but the attorneys at my old law office kept me informed as to what was going on. Even though I was elected to the city court, I supported getting more Blacks elected to the bench in Baton Rouge and around the state.

Local motivation to challenge the at-large system of electing judges in Baton Rouge grew out of a similar challenge in Mississippi. In *Kirksey v. Allain*, Black lawyers filed suit in federal district court in Mississippi, challenging the system of electing circuit, chancery, and some county court judges. They alleged that the multimember at-large system of electing judges in Mississippi diluted Black voting strength and violated Section 2 of the Voting Rights Act of 1965, 42 U.S.C. §1973. Attorneys Clark, Bell, Ernest Johnson, and others approached Robert McDuff, an attorney with the Lawyers Committee for Civil Rights and a lead attorney in the

Mississippi case, about filing a similar suit in Louisiana. They all felt that a Section 2 claim was applicable to East Baton Rouge Parish and the State of Louisiana as a whole. I reiterated my suggestion that they might fare better by not including the City of Baton Rouge and the city court in their lawsuit. Our conversation preceded the eventual filing of *Clark v. Edwards* in the Federal District Court for the Middle District of Louisiana.

Several changes had taken place on the Nineteenth Judicial District Court for the parish of East Baton Rouge since my election on March 26, 1983. At least three seats on the district bench opened up, creating opportunities for new judges, yet there were still no Black judges on that court. In September 1984 Norbert Rayford, who had made an unsuccessful run for the city court, filed for a district court seat and was the first to qualify for Division B of the Nineteenth Judicial District. He drew opposition from Bob Downing. Norbert had served as judicial commissioner for the Nineteenth Judicial District Court for a couple of years. He believed that his experience as commissioner could help level the playing field in a race where the demographics did not favor a Black candidate. African Americans made up only 31 percent of the voting population in the parish, which put him at a distinct disadvantage. But again, as in his city court race, the demographics and polarized voting brought about another agonizing loss to Downing.

In 1986 Janice Clark filed to run for an open seat on the Nineteenth Judicial District Court. After filing her qualifying papers, she and several other Black lawyers, including Norbert Rayford, marched over to the Federal District Court for the Middle District of Louisiana and filed the lawsuit that came to be known as *Clark v. Edwards*. Like *Kirksey v. Allain* in Mississippi, the Louisiana lawsuit challenged the at-large voting system for judges in East Baton Rouge Parish. As expected, Janice's run for the district court was likewise unsuccessful. Still, it provided additional evidence of polarized voting and demonstrated how difficult it was for African Americans to win at-large judicial elections in East Baton Rouge.

I was ready and well equipped to move up to the district court. I already had four and a half years of judicial experience serving on the Baton

Rouge City Court. Also, I received extensive training at both the National and Louisiana Judicial Colleges. My experience, training, and ad hoc appointment to the Nineteenth Judicial District Court convinced me that I was ready to make a move.

I asked political consultant David Roach to examine the demographics of a district court race and analyze what it would take for me to win. This race was a parish-wide endeavor and would be a momentous undertaking, vastly different from the single-ballot-issue race I ran for the city court. There would inevitably be several other local and statewide races on the ballot that would increase the voter turnout. Moreover, the demographic makeup of the cities of Baker and Zachary, plus the unincorporated area known as Central, which was two-thirds white and had a history of polarized voting, was going to be a factor. David surmised that we would need to outperform white voter turnout in the Black precincts and capture at least 25 percent of the white vote.

## Putting the Campaign Team Back Together

I needed to know if I could get my old campaign team together to support me in another run for the next-highest court—the Nineteenth Judicial District Court. I met with the attorneys at my former law office on Plank Road and told them I was thinking about running for the district court. I let it be known to the members of the Louis A. Martinet Society that I would run. I met with Chick Moore, Ed Walters, Lennie Perez, John Noland, and Michael Patterson, all of whom had played a significant role in my successful city court election. Press Robinson, my former campaign manager, agreed to serve again.

I made my way over to the Chicken Shack to discuss my intentions with Joe Delpit. I was surprised to learn that the attorney representing Joe in a matter before the Nineteenth Judicial District Court was also contemplating a district court run and had asked Delpit to back him instead of me. This attorney stoked the prevailing notion that a Black candidate running against a white candidate could not win a parish-wide race. After discussing both demographics and strategy, I left knowing that once again I had Joe's support. I also visited with my ministerial team of Rev. Ulysses Hayes and Rev. Lionel Lee, and they both agreed to help again.

I was hoping a seat would open on district court as a result of the retirement of one of the older judges. However, the untimely death of Judge John Covington of the Louisiana First Circuit Court of Appeal put the possibility of an open seat on the district court into play sooner than expected. Frank Foil, chief judge of the Nineteenth Judicial District Court, announced that he would run for Judge Covington's seat on the First Circuit. With his anticipated win, the door would swing wide open for lawyers to vie for his seat on the district court. Members of the bar began speculating and maneuvering to see who would capture Judge Foil's seat if he moved up to the First Circuit. The *Morning Advocate* ran an article on July 11, 1987, noting that Assistant District Attorneys Dennis Weber and Prem Burns indicated that they planned on leaving the District Attorney's Office to seek a judgeship. The same article included my name as a potential candidate for Judge Foil's seat if he successfully claimed the First Circuit Court of Appeal seat. It became apparent that I would not have the luxury of moving to the next-highest level in the court system without opposition, as had at least four of my predecessors on the city court. Another glass ceiling confronted me.

I happened to stop at Alford's Safe and Lock store to have a key made several days after the *Morning Advocate*'s article about potential district court candidates when Prem Burns walked in. We had always been cordial, and I considered her a friend ever since we had worked together when Ossie Brown was the DA. She was a misdemeanor assistant then, whereas I handled felony trials. On this day at Alford's Safe and Lock, however, Prem avoided me.

Since my departure from the District Attorney's Office ten years earlier, Prem Burns's career as an assistant district attorney had skyrocketed. She became one of the top prosecutors in the office. She achieved national notoriety when she successfully prosecuted three Colombians for the contract killing of "Barry" Seal, an undercover informant for the Drug Enforcement Administration and a participant in the sting that helped prove the Sandinistas were involved in dealing cocaine. Seal, who also was a pilot and drug smuggler for the Medellín Cartel, a Colombian cocaine enterprise, was expected to be a key witness against Colombian drug lord Pablo Escobar Gaviria before his death. Prem, a white female

Republican with high visibility and demographic advantage, would be a formidable opponent.

I received a call from an attorney, whom I will call Robert for the purposes of this memoir. He supported me for city court and asked for a meeting. Robert wanted to discuss Judge Foil's seat on the district court, assuming there was no opposition to Foil's move up to the First Circuit. In addition to being a lawyer, Robert also held a Ph.D. in political science and had been a university professor before entering full-time practice. His viewpoint was well worth considering.

We agreed to meet at Chick Moore's office. I called Press Robinson and asked him to attend. Robert arrived, accompanied by another attorney, whom I will refer to as Theo. To my surprise, Robert began by saying that I should reconsider running for the district bench because I couldn't possibly win a parish-wide election since the odds were so firmly against me. He started to break down the numbers, and I told him I already knew the numbers. He suggested that I defer to Theo, a well-respected white attorney with a sizable African American clientele. I reiterated, "I am running for the district court." He tried to change my mind by referring to both Baker's and Zachary's inhospitable demographics. I again told him I was familiar with those areas and the challenges I faced. Robert thanked me for my time, and as they were leaving, he said, "Fred, you can't win parish-wide." When reviewing the final list of lawyers who had signed onto my committee to elect me to the district court, I found both Robert and Theo's names among them.

My media advisor shared a conversation with a friend who purported to be an expert in political campaigning. The gist of their discussion was that a litany of things would work against me in a parish-wide race. First, he believed that I couldn't win, and if I did, it would be inadvisable to put my picture on any campaign material distributed in Baker, Zachary, and Central. That seemed ludicrous to me since I had been all over the parish for the past four and a half years, attending public events as Judge Freddie Pitcher of the Baton Rouge City Court. I had already appeared at numerous events sponsored by Mayor Pete Heine of Baker, including his annual prayer breakfast, which was well attended and covered by the media. Hundreds of people appeared in my court over the last four and a half years who lived outside the city limits and saw, beyond a doubt, that I was Black. It would be absurd for me to try to hide the fact that I am Black. I am who I am, and if I couldn't win based upon my record, I didn't want the job.

Running a parish-wide race meant campaigning in Baker, Zachary, and the unincorporated area known as Central. All three were predominantly white and reputedly very conservative, which put me at a demographic disadvantage. African Americans made up approximately 31 percent of the population in the parish. Nonetheless, I firmly believed I had a strong chance at victory.

Considering the challenges I faced in Baker, Zachary, and Central, my campaign team of advisors thought we should again organize separate campaign committees with distinct strategies for the Black and white communities, just as we did for my city court race. Our Black community strategy would be bottom-up, focusing on churches, street canvassing, media-specific messaging, phone banking, and mailgrams. Our plan for the white community would be top-down and concentrate on seeking endorsements from prominent and high-profile white politicians, including the mayors of Baker and Zachary. In Central, our target politician was State Representative Donald Ray Kennard, whose district included that area. Kennard was a member of the Democratic Party at the time. Getting the endorsement of former mayor W. W. "Woody" Dumas, who lived in Baker and had ties all over the parish, would bolster my campaign significantly.

Mayor Dumas knew me from my days as federal aid coordinator for the city-parish. I had represented him at several meetings in Baton Rouge and Washington, D.C. Mayor Pete Heine of Baker and I became friends through my participation in his annual prayer breakfasts. Zachary mayor John Womack was in law enforcement before taking office and knew me from my days as an assistant district attorney. Representative Kennard was the only one I didn't know well, and I needed Joe Delpit to intercede on my behalf.

I thought that getting a commitment from Mayor Dumas would help me secure Heine's, Womack's, and Kennard's endorsements. To get Mayor Dumas on board, I called on Cleve Taylor, a friend of mine and a former executive assistant to Mayor Dumas, and asked him to arrange a meeting. I knew that if Cleve approached him, Dumas would meet with me. The mayor was very gracious. He told me he had followed my career and thought I was doing a great job. I told him I was running for the Nineteenth Judicial District Court and hoped to get his endorsement. He asked who else was running, and I replied, "Prem Burns." He asked me to draft an endorsement letter, and if he liked it, he would sign it. I told him that we were also hoping to get Mayor Heine's endorsement and asked if he had any objection to signing off on a joint letter. Dumas replied, "If Pete's okay, I am okay."

Mayor Heine was also very welcoming and happy to receive my visit. I told him that I was running for a seat on the Nineteenth Judicial District Court and hoped to get his support. I told him that Mayor Dumas was already on board, and I hoped he would consider endorsing me as well. My campaign was preparing a letter for Mayor Dumas to sign and asked if he would co-sign it. He told me if I had Woody's endorsement, I had his as well.

I contacted Mayor Womack of Zachary and offered the same pitch I had made to Mayor Dumas and Mayor Heine. Mayor Womack, however, declined to sign off on a joint letter. He said he would support me, but he wanted to write his own letter of endorsement. Getting his support was critical, and a separate letter from him would significantly impact his constituents in Zachary.

Then I contacted Representative Kennard, whose district covered Central. He was also an academic advisor to LSU's athletic department and a spotter for the LSU Sports Radio Network. After making contact, he invited me to meet with him at his parents' home one morning for coffee. Representative Kennard was a Democrat and indicated that he would support me in my bid for the district court, but he wanted me to meet his father, a justice of the peace in the Central area. If his father placed my yard sign on his property, I was told, the locals would notice. We had our meeting, and before leaving, his father put my campaign sign in his front yard.

Representative Kennard told me about a "meet the candidates" rally that was to be held in the Central High School gymnasium on the following Saturday and suggested I attend. Central was reputed to have vestiges of the Ku Klux Klan therein and nearby and was an area not known to be welcoming to Blacks. I had a little angst about attending the event, but I told Representative Kennard I would come. Not wanting to go alone, I convinced Ed Walters to accompany me. He likewise had a bit of angst about going. When we arrived, we found the gym full of white residents. I had a handful of my push cards, as did Ed, but the all-white crowd, I believe, was a little intimidating, and Ed decided to stay by the door. I walked into the bleachers and passed out my push cards, saying, "I would appreciate your vote on November 21." Some of the folks accepted my push card; others declined.

A gray-haired and long-bearded white gentleman stopped me and asked for one of my cards. He told me that he was in my court when I presided over a case involving his son and felt I was a fair man. He said, "I am going to vote for you, and I am going to get my friends, who were sitting next to me, to vote for you." I thanked him, passed out a few more cards, and made my way out of the gym, encouraged that I might get some voters from Central to back me.

My campaign disseminated the endorsements I received through an attractive trifold campaign mailer sent to targeted homes in the white community. The trifold included the endorsements of the *State-Times* and *Morning Advocate* newspapers; retired judges Eugene McGehee and Lewis Doherty; former mayor of East Baton Rouge Parish Woody Dumas; Baker mayor Pete Heine; and Zachary mayor John Womack. It also included endorsements from Champac, the political arm of the Chamber of Commerce, the Alliance for Good Government, Labor Union Local 1177, and a notation that more than 250 lawyers endorsed my candidacy.

Judge Foil ascended to the Louisiana First Circuit Court of Appeal's open seat, removing that contest from the September 21 primary. Governor Edwin Edwards called an election for November 4 to fill the vacant seat on the Nineteenth Judicial District Court. I got a surprise telephone call from Mayor Pat Screen suggesting that I ask the governor to include the district court race in the February 1988 Super Tuesday election. I felt uncomfortable putting this race off for another three months as it might draw more challengers. Pat Screen felt Super Tuesday would maximize the Black voter turnout for me. If my election were part of Super Tuesday, it might help pass other items the mayor favored on the ballot as well. I discussed the mayor's suggestions with my campaign team. They opposed the delay, so I told Mayor Screen that I wouldn't make the ask. I later learned he was pretty angry at my refusal to take his advice.

As our campaign progressed, voter support in the Black community solidified, but my success hinged upon maximizing voter turnout parish-wide. I intended to be equally aggressive in seeking Black and white votes. Judging from Norbert Rayford's district court race in particular, it would be a challenge to get 25 percent of the white vote. A concentrated effort to appeal to that demographic was needed.

### The Campaign Strategy

Even though I had run a well-organized and professional city court campaign, this campaign needed to be far more sophisticated and expansive. When I ran for the city court, we only used radio stations catering primarily to Black audiences. Likewise, our print media primarily targeted the Black community. But this race was different. I needed to highlight my qualifications using every avenue of outreach I could muster, including polished television advertisements, all of which required money.

My fundraising strategy included my making a loan to the "Freddie Pitcher for District Court" campaign. I learned early that potential donors expect a candidate to contribute to his own election before they decide to donate. I thought that twenty-five thousand dollars would be enough to start. My friend John Noland volunteered to run interference with the loan officer at City National Bank for me.

I met with the loan officer whom John contacted, and he was eager to help. He wanted to know how much I needed. We opened a campaign account with twenty-five thousand dollars and began our media blitz targeting both the Black and white communities. Based on what I had seen in previous elections, losing candidates often had difficulty raising money to pay off loans made to finance their campaigns. I didn't have twenty-five thousand dollars to do that, so winning was imperative.

On August 7, 1987, Chick Moore, Ed Walters, and Lennie Perez sent out the following letter to members of the Baton Rouge Bar Association:

Dear Fellow Attorney:

Now that Judge Foil has been elected to the First Circuit Court of Appeal, the governor has set the election to fill his vacancy on the 19th Judicial District Court for November 21, 1987.

Support for Judge Pitcher's candidacy to fill Judge Foil's seat has been overwhelming. As can be seen from Judge Pitcher's qualifications, which are enclosed, the legal community has recognized that he is the best person for the job.

A month ago, our committee had 28 members; it now numbers 250. To underscore the broad base of support for Judge Pitcher, we would like to include you on our list of committee members. Call the committee at 343–8346 and let us know of your support, and we will welcome you as a member. Or, if you prefer, sign the bottom of the letter and drop it in the mail.

Working together, we will assure a resounding victory for Judge Pitcher in November.

Very truly yours
JUDGE PITCHER FOR
DISTRICT COURT COMMITTEE

The committee's letter resulted in several very successful fundraising events leading up to the November 21 election.

The first of our planned fundraisers was a *cochon de lait* in Ed and Norma Walters's backyard at their luxurious new home. Congressman Billy Tauzin served as the guest chef for the event. He was looking at a run for governor. Some thought having Representative Tauzin as guest chef would help sell tickets to our event. I alerted some friends, who were Governor Edwin Edwards supporters, that Tauzin's participation in this event was not my endorsement of his candidacy for governor but rather a fundraising ploy of my finance committee.

A *cochon de lait* involves roasting a pig over an open hardwood fire and is a very festive event in South Louisiana. We sent invitations to all Baton Rouge Bar Association members, pricing the event at one hundred dollars per couple.

Our caterer provided a pig that weighed more than three hundred pounds. It took four of us to lift it from the truck using a long iron rod that impaled the pig from end to end. We set it onto a rotisserie known as a "Cajun microwave." Attorney Burton Guidry's high-velocity Cajun and Zydeco band performed at the event. Many friends and supporters came, which added more than ten thousand dollars to our campaign coffers.

We held our next fundraiser at the home of Lewis and Gail Unglesby. The Unglesbys' house sat high on a hill about fifty yards from the street. Two well-known chefs catered. All we had to do was provide the ingredients they requested. Between 350 and 400 people came. Cars were parked all over the Unglesbys' yard, down their driveway to the street, and onto Highland Road for at least a quarter of a mile. The event spoke volumes about the overall diversity of my campaign and again raised a significant sum of money.

November 21, 1987, was the official election date for the district court seat I was seeking, as well as for other elective offices, including that of the governor, providing there was no outright winner in the October primary. I made my way to the secretary of state's office on the first day of qualifying and filed to run for the district court seat. I was pretty confident that Prem Burns would run, but I was surprised to learn that Dennis Weber didn't file. Much had been made of his leaving the District Attorney's Office for the race, and I always assumed I would have two opponents instead of one. I don't know why he changed his mind, but this turn of events benefited me considerably. I was now able to direct all of my resources toward the general election.

I wanted to start my campaign by announcing my intention to run for the district court to all the Black pastors and ministers who made up the East Baton Rouge Ministerial Alliance. Having a chance to speak before their church congregations was a great way to reach large groups of potential voters. Hopefully, my message and the cause would be enough to get parishioners motivated to vote on election day. It had proved to be a winning strategy for my city court election and became a significant part of our strategy for the district court. Today, however, political candidates might be acknowledged but likely not offered a chance to speak to congregations because churches might jeopardize their tax-exempt status if they were perceived to be involved in politics.

With the help of the Reverends Lee, Hayes, and Charles T. Smith, I attended a fellowship prayer breakfast at the Shiloh Missionary Baptist Church. Church leaders from all over East Baton Rouge Parish attended.

I thanked everyone for coming and for their prayers and support over the past four and a half years. I asked them to continue and help me become the first African American elected to the Nineteenth Judicial District Court. I told them that all of the political pundits were saying that demographically I couldn't win because Blacks made up only 31 percent of the population in the parish. We proved them wrong in 1983, I said, and with their prayers, votes, support, and the support of their congregations, I hoped to prove the naysayers wrong a second time.

I told them that of the two candidates vying for the district court judge position, I was the only one with judicial experience. It is also important to note that the Louisiana Supreme Court appointed me on two separate occasions to serve as a district court judge ad hoc on the Nineteenth Judicial District Court.

I explained my campaign strategy and announced that Reverend Hayes and Reverend Lee would be getting in touch with them in the coming days to arrange for me to visit and hopefully address their congregations.

Regrettably, Black political organizations had little time to devote to my campaign. They all were heavily involved in Governor Edwin Edwards's reelection efforts or the efforts of one of his challengers. The gubernatorial challengers were U.S. Representatives Robert Livingston and Billy Tauzin, Secretary of State Jim Brown, and U.S. Representative Buddy Roemer. The primary for the gubernatorial race was October 24, 1987. I attended every meeting my scheduler could arrange for me between the primary and the general election. I was giving speeches and making meetings from one end of the parish to the other. I frequented the campaign events of candidates running for many other state and local government positions, especially if their voters also voted in my race. The goal was to mingle while wearing my "Pitcher for District Court" badge, and if appropriate, pass out my election push card.

We set up campaign headquarters in an office on Main Street. The building's front area provided an ideal workspace for volunteers. We added several additional lines to enhance our phone bank capacity. We also had a large conference room suitable for volunteers to use for stuffing campaign mailers. My daughter Kyla, who was in the tenth grade at Baton Rouge High, was eager to get involved. She recruited a number of her classmates to volunteer. They came in on several Saturdays to stuff and label envelopes. We were pleased to have such a diverse group of Kyla's friends and fellow students from Baton Rouge High help out.

The building's rear warehouse became the hub of our sign production operation. The same team that handled signage for my first court campaign came aboard. After putting in a full day at their regular jobs, they stopped by every evening to work the silk-screening apparatus to make our large wooden signs.

The individual who coordinated my headquarters operations for the city court election had moved out of town. I desperately needed someone to manage our day-to-day campaign headquarters operations, especially since I was a sitting judge with a full docket and could not get to headquarters until late afternoon. Lt. Col. Harold Webb, a retired army officer, volunteered.

Colonel Webb had been one of my students in law school. He stopped by one evening to see how he might be of assistance. He helped map out a logistical game plan as if he were still active military. His organizational skills were a godsend.

On the night of the gubernatorial primary election, the whole state was shocked when Governor Edwin Edwards announced that he was dropping out of the race after coming in second place, ceding the governorship to Buddy Roemer. The latter led the field with 33 percent of the vote. What a bombshell! The lack of a gubernatorial race on the November 21 ballot would invariably impact voter turnout. We were counting on the governor's race to bring out a large turnout in the African American community, which would have inured to my benefit. With only down-ballot races remaining, we wondered if there would be enough excitement among voters to bring my base out to the polls. This turn of events meant that we had to intensify our parish-wide efforts. I began to wonder whether I had made a mistake by not asking the governor to schedule the district court election on Super Tuesday as Mayor Pat Screen had suggested.

Another shock came with the unexpected defeat of State Senator Richard "Dick" Turnley, who lost to Cleo Fields, a twenty-four-year-old recent law school graduate and former student of mine. Cleo stopped by one of my fundraisers, brought a rather sizable campaign contribution, and committed his support and that of his entire campaign team, including his super get-out-the-vote (GOTV) operations. His efforts helped shore up our outreach in North Baton Rouge.

I began attending every event I could to increase my visibility. I made my first appearance with Prem Burns at a campaign forum before a predominantly white audience. When asked to speak, I deferred to Prem, saying, "ladies first." Prem attempted to diminish my city court judicial experience while touting her felony trial experience, saying that the city court only dealt with misdemeanors. In contrast, the district court dealt with first-degree and second-degree murder cases, which she had handled for several years. When I got a chance to speak, I told the crowd that Ms. Burns had a short memory. I was a felony assistant in the District Attorney's Office when she was merely a misdemeanor assistant. She also failed to mention that I prosecuted the first capital murder trial in East Baton Rouge Parish after *Furman v. Georgia*, the U.S. Supreme Court case that reinstated the death penalty. I also noted that I was appointed a district court judge ad hoc on two separate occasions by appointment of the Louisiana Supreme Court.

I assured the crowd that my city court experience enabled me to better appreciate and understand the human dynamics of judging people, which one doesn't get simply from being a prosecutor. Prem never again tried to diminish my qualifications when we appeared together. She did, however, put out a comparison flyer with her photo and qualifications and my photo and no qualifications.

Running a parish-wide race was time-consuming and intense. I often found myself traveling from one end of the parish to the other. Judy Bethley, my scheduler, set up speaking events or appearances morning, noon, and night. Most were small events reaching twenty or fewer voters. Every Saturday I put up signs or walked neighborhoods. I visited nearly every Black beauty parlor and barbershop in the parish, leaving emery boards with "Pitcher for District Court" printed on them. Sundays I was on the church circuit, visiting anywhere from three to four churches and allowed to address the congregations.

With the election just a few days away, Press Robinson and I contacted Joe Delpit to check on the parish-wide coordinated GOTV operations. All the Black political organizations had met and agreed to issue a uniform ballot endorsing my candidacy for the Nineteenth Judicial District Court. They also decided not to assess any cost to me for doing so as they had during my city court race.

I thought we had all the Black political organizations covered until City Councilwoman Pearl George, who had agreed not to ask for funds for her political organization, told me she needed help to pay her campaign workers. She told me she might not be able to handle her assigned canvassing area without some additional financial assistance. I needed every foot soldier I could muster to encourage our constituents to get out and vote. I negotiated her down from her initial ask and instructed my campaign treasurer to cut her a check. The canvassing effort of Councilwoman George's group was well worth the money she asked from me.

In addition to numerous personal speaking engagements, I saturated the radio the last few days of the campaign with thirty-second radio spots. Our GOTV canvassers walked the neighborhoods, leaving push cards and encouraging people to go to the polls on November 21. To boost our campaign efforts, my campaign released a television commercial, a first for a Black candidate, a few days before the election, highlighting my credentials and achievements.

# 6

# Elected

*Judge of the Nineteenth Judicial District Court*

I SPENT ELECTION DAY traveling around the parish checking on precinct voter turnout. David Roach kept close tabs on the reports coming in from our poll watchers and felt we were in an excellent position to pull off another victory. Turnout in the predominantly Black precincts had been steady all day, which gave us confidence that my long-shot candidacy had a real chance. By the end of the day, I was exhausted and looked forward to heading off to the hotel, where we would await the returns and hopefully celebrate our victory.

Despite all of David Roach's assurances that I had won, I had an unsettling feeling. The suspense of the election outcome while waiting for 226 precincts to report created a lot of anxiety, and I knew it wouldn't go away until I got the official word from election officials that I had won. Harriet and Kyla were similarly affected.

Prem and I ran neck and neck throughout the early reporting. In my city court race, Kyla had started to cry when I fell behind, thinking that I would lose, until Louis Hamilton explained to her that the late reporting would likely work in our favor. This time there was no such drama from Kyla when we fell behind. She acted like a seasoned campaign veteran, knowing that our fortunes would change when the Black precincts began reporting.

In the end, I received 42,671 votes, which represented 52 percent of the votes cast. It also was most gratifying to learn that I picked up nearly 40 percent of the white votes in this election. My victory against the odds was decisive.

Before celebrating, Louis Hamilton led us in prayer. My supporters poured into the ballroom from all over the parish to join us in our victory party. It was an incredible evening. Like before, the night was exhausting but quite satisfying.

The following morning, Harriet, Kyla, and I went to church as usual. We got the same royal treatment Pastor Francois and the congregation at Belfair Baptist had given us after my city court election. Even though it had been nearly five years since my election to the city court, Black folks were every bit as excited with this win as they were after my first campaign.

My investiture ceremony took place at the Riverside Centroplex, which had a theater for the performing arts with a seating capacity of approximately two thousand people. The theater was almost full. The African American community came out en masse, as did many of my white friends and supporters. Louisiana Supreme Court Associate Justice Luther Cole administered the oath of office. He told the audience that he first met me when I was a law school student and knew then that my knowledge of the law would take me as far as I wanted to go. This investiture ceremony was a moving moment for me, and I had to work hard to maintain my composure.

I was sworn in as a district court judge on December 14, 1987, with a ceremonial investiture of office on January 2, 1988, joining twelve other judges on the district court bench. I was assigned to hear criminal cases in Section I of the court. I had no qualms with the assignment because I felt my background as an assistant district attorney and criminal defense lawyer would enable me to hit the ground running. Within days of my investiture, I was on the job. The first order of business was to serve as the duty judge for the Christmas holidays. As the duty judge, I had to review and sign search and arrest warrants, set bonds, and handle jail callouts of persons arrested who couldn't make bonds. There's an old saying that "stuff rolls downhill." The assignment rolled down to me as the new and "junior" judge. I had no say-so in this holiday assignment.

I found a hefty backlog of billed and unbilled cases in my new criminal court section requiring my immediate attention. The buildup stemmed from my predecessor, who had a penchant for what some called "creative" sentencing. He would order special conditions for probation that were often difficult to meet. The defendants' poverty and limited education often made it challenging for them to meet some of the unique conditions he imposed. Nevertheless, the judge ordered defendants back to court repeatedly for reviews, causing the docket to balloon. He was well-intentioned, but it was my job to clean up what he left behind when he moved to the civil side of the district court.

I modified the terms and conditions of probation for many defendants, which made it easier for them to complete and reduced the likelihood of their facing probation revocation and jail. The move also cut down on the number of times defendants had to report back for review, which helped unclog the docket.

I immersed myself in managing a backlogged schedule while simultaneously working through all the new cases that flooded the court. Since many defendants with felony charges were stuck in jail because they could not make bond, I put extra effort into pushing their cases through the system. The assistant district attorney and assistant public defender assigned to my court worked out plea agreements for many of the defendants, which gave them credit for time served and made them eligible for release. During my first two years on the bench, I ranked either first or second for having the highest number of cases disposed of by jury trials, and I remained near the top during my entire tenure on the Nineteenth Judicial District Court.

Of all the cases I presided over as a district court judge, three stood out and stuck with me the most. The first one was the *State of Louisiana v. Howard E. Rollins Jr.;* the defendant was an acclaimed actor from the television series *In the Heat of the Night.* The second was the *State of Louisiana v. Dewitt O'Neal Sanders and Joby Vaughn Letard,* which involved a senseless act that took the life of a young woman and resulted in an unprecedented show of forgiveness. The third was the *State of Louisiana v. Feltus Taylor,* in which the defendant was indicted for first-degree murder, tried, and found guilty by a jury.

## State of Louisiana v. Howard E. Rollins Jr.

On Sunday, March 27, 1988, during my second rotation as duty judge, I got a call from the court's bail bond coordinator at East Baton Rouge Parish Prison to set a bond on a man named Howard E. Rollins Jr. for possession of cocaine, DWI, and driving 100 mph in a 55-mph speed zone. Though the name sounded familiar, I didn't think much of it at the time. Our bond coordinator recommended a bond of five thousand dollars, suggesting the amount was standard for first offenders.

The following day, while sitting in chambers reviewing the stack of probable cause affidavits for weekend arrests, I took a closer look at the Rollins affidavit. I wondered if this might be the same person who starred in the television series *In the Heat of the Night*. Drilling down a little more, I concluded that it was, in fact, the actor, who was on location filming the series in Hammond, Louisiana. I couldn't believe it! Detective Virgil Tibbs was caught up in a real-life situation in the criminal justice system in Baton Rouge, Louisiana. I was an avid fan of Rollins—a two-time nominee for best supporting actor in the movies *Ragtime* and *A Soldier's Story*. I also watched the television series. As I mused about his situation, I realized that he could very well be facing his own *In the Heat of the Night* episode with these charges.

The affidavit of probable cause stated the following: On March 27, 1988, at 2:24 a.m., a Louisiana state policeman clocked the Rollins vehicle going more than 95 mph in a 45-mph zone on I-12 east of Sherwood Forest Boulevard. He was also clocked driving at a speed of 100+ mph in a 55-mph zone east of O'Neal Lane. Rollins's vehicle weaved onto the shoulder a couple of times. The trooper stopped the vehicle on I-12 east of O'Neal. The affidavit further stated that a Black male carefully exited the vehicle, took off a yellow leather jacket, and laid it on the trunk of the car. Rollins was unsteady on his feet and had a strong odor of alcoholic beverage about his person. The trooper noted in the affidavit that Rollins did very poorly on the field sobriety test, so he placed Rollins under arrest. After arresting Rollins, the state trooper found two bags of white powder (cocaine) in Rollins's coat pocket. The subject was given his rights and taken to Troop A headquarters. His 0.15 percent reading on an alcohol test led to his being charged with "driving while under the influence 1st offense." He was also charged with possession of cocaine, and speeding at 100+ mph in a 55-mph zone.

I later learned that Rollins posted a cash bond, was released, and was given notice of when he was to appear in my court.

The actor's arrest in Baton Rouge, Louisiana, was sure to hit the wire services and invariably draw much attention to his case in my court. As a brand-new district court judge and the only Black judge in Baton Rouge, I knew that I had to get ready for whatever might be coming my way.

After formal charges were filed against Mr. Rollins on June 9, 1988, through a bill of information, the next order of business was setting a date for his arraignment. The bill of information charged him with knowingly and intentionally possessing cocaine, a controlled dangerous substance. Separate bills were filed covering the "driving while under the influence of alcohol" and "speeding 100 mph in 55-mph zone" charges. Because these were all rather low-level offenses, the district attorney chose the bills of information route for bringing formal charges instead of taking this case to the grand jury. Rollins received notice through his attorney to appear in my court for arraignment on August 3, 1988.

Jim Boren, Rollins's local counsel, appeared without him at arraignment. I sensed I might have a little trouble getting Rollins to meet his court dates as scheduled. I wondered out loud if Mr. Rollins felt that his celebrity gave him special privileges, which meant he didn't have to come to court when summoned to do so. Boren assured me that this wasn't the case. Rollins's failure to appear was a mix-up with scheduling in his California office.

Boren motioned, without opposition from the District Attorney's Office, to continue the arraignment, which I granted and had him accept notice on behalf of his client for August 24, 1988. On August 24, I was presented with a notarized affidavit from Howard Rollins requesting that his presence be waived at his arraignment and that his plea of "not guilty" to all charges be made in absentia by attorney Jim Boren. I advised Mr. Boren that there would be no more waivers of appearances for his client, and I insisted that Mr. Rollins be in court on September 22, 1988, for status and motions.

So began a nearly two-year odyssey of working the *Howard Roll-ins* case through the court system in Baton Rouge. The tabloids had long speculated that the actor had an alcohol and drug problem. Folks hoped that the threat of a five-year prison sentence for the possession of cocaine charge would be the impetus Rollins needed to finally address his addictive behavior. This arrest, many believed, could put his career in jeopardy.

As the District Attorney's Office was trying to get Rollins's case to court, there was always some reason why the actor couldn't appear on the assigned date. I finally put my foot down and insisted that we get the case moving. I had reassigned it from September 22 to October 26 for motions and status. It was now at November 14—the absolute last straw.

A few days before the November 14, 1988, status conference, Jim Boren and Assistant District Attorney Glen Lorio met with me in my chambers and told me Rollins would be entering a guilty plea in his case. They told me that the District Attorney's Office had no objection to my imposing a sentence under Article 893 of the Louisiana Code of Criminal Procedure. Lorio said that Mr. Rollins was a first-time felony offender and had admitted himself to an in-patient alcohol and drug treatment facility after his arrest in Baton Rouge. Boren said that he had discussed the matter with his client and pleading guilty was the course of action Rollins wished to take. He presented a letter of support for Rollins from the Caron Foundation attesting to Rollins's completion of an in-patient treatment program for drugs and alcohol from April 16, 1988, to April 21, 1988. The letter stated that "Howard seems sincere about learning information about himself and his illness, and has committed himself to a continuing care program."

Boren presented another letter addressed to me from Edward Led-ding, producer of *In the Heat of the Night* (MGM/UA Television Productions, Inc.). Mr. Ledding's letter commented on the noticeable change that had taken place in Rollins since he completed the in-patient program at the Caron Foundation, noting that Rollins reported to the series production set on time and had an excellent work record. He also stated that even Rollins's thinking was clear and focused. The actor's dedication to "cleaning up his act" had earned Rollins the producer's respect.

Sentencing Rollins under Louisiana Code of Criminal Procedure Article 893 meant having his guilty plea set aside and the prosecution dismissed. For this to happen, however, he had to meet all of the terms and conditions of probation. If he did so, he also would have the opportunity for an expungement of his arrest record.

On November 14, 1988, Howard Rollins appeared in court with counsel, James "Jim" Boren, who advised me that Mr. Rollins wished to withdraw his "not guilty" plea and enter a plea of "guilty as charged." I asked Mr. Rollins if this was truly his desire, and he responded affirmatively. I had him sworn in and proceeded to carry him through the required Boykin Examination to ensure that he knowingly and intelligently waived his constitutional rights. After I carried him through the colloquy, I ruled that there was a factual basis for the prosecution, and I stated for the record that I believed that Howard Rollins understood the significance of his guilty plea and that he knowingly, intelligently, and voluntarily waived his right to plead not guilty. Thus, I accepted his plea of guilty to the charge of possession of cocaine. A similar examination was followed for the DWI charge, though it was not as extensive.

Rollins's attorney then advised the court that the actor wished to waive any delays and be sentenced that very day. Since I had been made aware of the possibility that he would make such a request, I devised a sentence that I hoped would get his attention and put him on the path to addressing his addiction. I stated, for the record, that his sentence was deferred under the provisions of Louisiana Revised Statute 40:893 for a period of two years and placed him on bench probation under the supervision of Phelps and Dalrymple Forensic Services, a private probation supervision service, which made it easier for him to meet the demands of his acting profession. The key components of the terms and conditions of his probation were periodic drug screening and analysis, performing 240 hours of community service in the form of participating in making an antidrug and substance abuse video, and paying some hefty fines.

The antidrug and substance abuse video was of particular interest, and I quickly bought into the idea when it was initially presented to me by Don Wydra, assistant secretary for juvenile services in the Louisiana Department of Public Safety and Corrections. The Department of Corrections would bear the cost of filming the video, provided that Rollins agreed to volunteer his services and had no contract prohibitions. It was an opportunity to use Howard Rollins's celebrity status to get a message out to youngsters about the evils of drugs and alcohol. Having him travel around the country to give antidrug and alcohol speeches was one thing, but having a well-made video running regularly on television would reach a far larger audience, and the video could be used indefinitely.

Approximately one year after his guilty plea, Rollins appeared back in my court for a scheduled review of his probation. Several months before that review, I saw the actor on a late-night television show. It was apparent he was under the influence of something. The host of the program was taking great delight in the instability of Rollins's condition. I shared this with Rollins's attorney and reminded him that Rollins's deferred sentence would be in jeopardy if he couldn't get his act together. I am sure Rollins and his team of handlers got my message because they quickly took proactive steps to get him back into treatment. At his probation review hearing, Mr. Rollins disclosed that he participated in a twenty-eight-day in-patient treatment program for alcohol abuse at the Betty Ford Treatment Center, a substance abuse clinic in California named for former president Gerald Ford's wife, who helped found it. His attorney told me that Rollins went in for treatment voluntarily because he believed he was drinking too much.

His stint at the Betty Ford Treatment Center was encouraging, though it wasn't enough to convince me that Rollins was out of the woods with his addiction. I extended his probation for an additional year and transferred his probation to Georgia, where he then lived, while filming his television series. After the hearing, I returned to my chambers, where my staff informed me that dozens of Rollins fans as well as many court employees had filed in to get autographs and have their photographs taken with the actor. I stepped out to take a look and observed the crowd's excitement at having a celebrity in their midst, regardless of what he had done that brought him there.

My subsequent encounter with Mr. Rollins resulted from a report that came out of the Georgia probation office. They notified me that Howard Rollins had missed office visits, failed to complete community service, and traveled outside the United States without prior approval. Rollins had also failed to provide monthly reports to probation and parole and was seriously behind on paying his supervision fees after being placed on probation. As a result, I ordered that Howard Rollins be given notice of a probation revocation hearing to determine whether I should revoke his probation and impose a sentence.

The notice of a probation revocation hearing got the attention of the manager and producers of the TV series. Reports began to roll in that Mr. Rollins had made a concerted effort to complete all of the conditions of probation, including paying his fines. I received a letter from Herb Adelman, a co-producer of *In the Heat of the Night,* that said, "through February of 1990, when the 1989–1990 production season ended, and again this past June, when Mr. Rollins had his medical exam for cast insurance, there was no evidence of any substance abuse." Also, the video we were waiting for finally got done. I received a copy, which proved to be an outstanding piece of work, sending the kind of anti–substance abuse message to the youngsters we hoped for. Rollins's thirty-second public service announcements started running on television stations in Baton Rouge immediately and were later released to stations in Georgia.

The video depicted a group of young children, ranging between ten and fifteen years old, sitting around as Rollins showed them several beautifully wrapped gift boxes. Rollins asks them to "pick one." Each of the kids picks a package. One has pills in it; one contains a bag of a white powdery substance; and the last contains a liquor bottle. Rollins then asks them: "Is this what you want? Are you certain? It's a pretty package. It's what I thought I wanted, but that's only the beginning. Let me tell you the whole story." He then discusses the terrible price that substance abuse exacts, using his own experience as an example.

The video aired for months, and it got rave reviews.

On November 13, 1990, Howard E. Rollins appeared before me for the final time. In this hearing, I reviewed his probation record. Although there were a few hiccups along the way, I determined he had fulfilled the terms and conditions of his probation. He had no other convictions during his probationary period, nor did he have any charges pending against him. Therefore, I ordered his convictions be set aside and that the prosecutions be dismissed in accordance with Louisiana Revised Statute 40:983.

In closing his case, I told him I hoped he truly learned the lessons he was imparting in his substance abuse videos. I wished him well and adjourned court, leaving him to an avalanche of fans seeking his autograph.

Although I was a fan of his, I had a job to do and wasn't inclined to go easy on him just because of who he was. Justice in my court had to be even-handed. I believe the actions we took to encourage him to pursue a healthier lifestyle may have helped to prolong what turned out to be a life that ended way too soon.

### State of Louisiana v. Dewitt O'Neal Sanders and Joby Vaughn Letard

The *Sanders and Letard* case involved two seventeen-year-old white youths out to have some "fun" by tossing several large pieces of concrete from a bridge over the interstate, impacting several cars below. One of those pieces of concrete crashed through the windshield of a vehicle driven by twenty-eight-year-old Diane Upp Simino, killing her instantly and injuring one other person. Sanders and Letard were arrested and charged with one count of manslaughter and three counts of aggravated criminal damage to property. What struck me about this case was the kindness and forgiveness exhibited by the decedent's family, something highly unusual in homicide cases. In most instances family and friends clamored for retribution in the sternest of ways.

The victim was the daughter of Dr. James Upp, a local pediatrician and chief of staff at Our Lady of the Lake Hospital. She was employed at the YMCA and was highly regarded by all. Her death was a tragic loss, as are most unexpected and untimely deaths. Still, during a sentencing hearing, Dr. Upp and his daughter Terri Upp Manning, Diane's sister, favored a sentence that would serve more to rehabilitate the young men than to punish them for their crimes, advocating no jail time at one point. Dr. Upp and Terri Upp Manning arranged to meet the two young men through their attorney to try to understand their motivation for the rock-throwing incident. Dr. Upp told me that after they met with the young men, they felt that this was nothing more than a prank that had gotten out of hand. When addressing the court, Terri Manning specifically recommended that I sentence Sanders and Letard to an Intensive Motivational Program of Alternative Correctional Treatment (IMPACT), a military-style boot camp at Hunt Correctional Center in St. Gabriel, Louisiana. The average length of stay for those who complete the program is between three to six months. The Department of Probation and Parole, however, did not recommend IMPACT for either Sanders or Letard in its presentence report.

At the time of this incident there was a robust daily discussion about it in the African American community on a radio talk show called *Question of the Day* that aired on WXOK. The talk show brought up the *Sanders and Letard* case frequently and speculated on what would happen to African American youths if they committed the same egregious and deadly prank. Listeners believed that Black youth in similar situations would be charged with more severe crimes and receive harsher sentences. Most of the callers seemed to know that I was the presiding judge, and their resentment came off as a subliminal message to me to punish these two white youths to the full extent of the law. Genevieve Stewart, the program host, was adept at firing up her listening audience. For the most part, her program was quite informative and focused on cutting-edge topics that kept her listeners highly engaged.

Being a product of the same community, I understood her audience's concerns. I, too, had witnessed some of the same things the callers discussed on the program. There was frustration in a community that had long been subjected to disparate treatment by the criminal justice system. Genevieve's radio show gave them a medium through which they could express their frustrations. As the presiding judge in the *Sanders and Letard* case, I was determined not to let a public outcry for retribution influence how I handled sentencing. Thankfully, I did not have Black youths before me in this case, but even if I did, they also would have been treated fairly and impartially, with dignity and respect like all who appear before me. This case was not about race but about the dire consequences of an egregious prank.

I received the presentencing investigation report from the Louisiana Division of Probation and Parole, which included sentencing recommendations. I heard all of the witnesses' and attorneys' allocutions. I wanted to give deference to the wishes of the victim's family for leniency as much as I could, but at the same time, I felt that jail time should be imposed. I thought it necessary for the sentence to serve as a deterrent, not only to the defendants themselves but also to those who might consider engaging in similar senseless acts.

I retired to my chambers to collect my thoughts and determine the sentence I intended to impose. I often told folks that the most challenging part of a judge's job was when the judge is alone in chambers agonizing over the appropriate sentence to impose upon a defendant.

Returning to a packed courtroom and calling the court to order, I directed the defendants to rise. As they stood with their attorneys, I began to read off their sentences. I told them in separate colloquies that they were sentenced to the custody of the secretary of the Louisiana Department of Corrections for seven years. I paused to let the psychological impact of their sentences take effect. Some folks in attendance gasped loudly. I then proceeded by telling them I was going to suspend the imposition of their sentence and place them both on probation for five years with the following conditions: (1) they each serve two years in the East Baton Rouge Parish Prison, credit for time served; (2) they each obtain their GEDs while incarcerated; (3) they each perform three hundred hours of community service at a hospital emergency room, youth-oriented program, or nursing home after release; (4) they each remain gainfully employed after release.

In addition to the sentence I imposed for the manslaughter charge, I sentenced them to three years imprisonment on the aggravated criminal damage to property charge, which sentence was to run concurrently with the sentence imposed on the manslaughter charge.

They had been incarcerated for several months in the East Baton Rouge Parish Prison and were entitled to credit for time served. They would likely spend only fifteen months in jail under the Department of Corrections' good behavior calculations.

This case stuck with me because of all the media attention it drew. I was forced to look deeper into my inner self and examine my own sense of humanity and forgiveness. I grew up in the church and believed in the Christian value of forgiveness. After witnessing so much murder and mayhem during my tenure as an assistant district attorney, a criminal defense lawyer, and now as a judge, I had to wonder if I had become hardened to its meaning. The unusual circumstance of having Dr. Upp and his daughter speak on behalf of these young men brought me back to my early lessons about what it meant to love your fellow man and how that played a part in forgiveness. The Upp family's act of forgiveness was a lesson in what "agape" means. Punishment, retribution, and rehabilitation, however, were not incongruent with forgiveness in this case.

### State of Louisiana v. Feltus Taylor

The *Feltus Taylor* case involved a charge of armed robbery, first-degree murder, and attempted murder.

On the morning of March 27, 1991, Feltus Taylor returned to Cajun's Fabulous Fried Chicken restaurant, from which he had been fired by manager Keith Clark weeks before. Taylor knocked on the back door. Clark recognized him and let him in. Their brief conversation included a request to be rehired, which Donna Ponsano, a former coworker, opposed. Taylor left the building and went to his car, retrieving a .22 caliber handgun and a pair of handcuffs. Upon returning, Taylor pulled the gun on Clark and Ponsano and made Clark open the safe, taking approximately eight hundred dollars. After handcuffing them together, he forced both of them into the restaurant's cooler. Taylor shot Ponsano first, then Clark, five times each, in the head. Ponsano died two days later. Clark survived but was paralyzed from the waist down.

The grand jury indicted Taylor for the first-degree murder of Donna Ponsano. The case was assigned to me as I was the judge on duty at the time the crime occurred. John Sinquefield, the chief assistant district attorney and my former boss when I was an assistant district attorney, took over the prosecution. Taylor was indigent and entitled to court-appointed counsel. I chose Bonnie Jackson, a public defender, and James "Jim" Boren, two outstanding criminal defense attorneys to represent him.

After weeks of motion practice and hearings, the case was ready for trial. A first-degree murder trial is probably the most delicate and intense trial of all. There is an excessive amount of pressure on all parties involved in a death penalty case like this—the judge, the jury, the prosecutor, and the defense counsel. Although I had prosecuted the first capital murder case in Baton Rouge years earlier, I felt the pressure of this case almost immediately. It fell upon me to manage the trial fairly and impartially for both the defendant and the prosecution, endeavoring not to commit any reversible errors in the process.

Under current law, capital or death penalty cases require that after being sworn in, jurors must be sequestered, subject to the caveat, "unless the state and the defense have jointly moved that the jury not be sequestered." Sequestration requires that jurors be kept together and secluded from outside communications throughout the course of the trial. It is stressful for them to be away from their families and loved ones for long periods, in addition to the burden of deciding the life-or-death fate of the defendant. I will take credit for the caveat as it emanated from the *Feltus Taylor* case.

Remembering the protracted jury selection process I had experienced during the capital case I had prosecuted years earlier and the toll it took on jurors, I thought it might lessen their burden and anxiety if they were not sequestered immediately. I reasoned that the way to avoid immediate sequestration was not to administer an oath immediately upon their selection but rather to instruct them not to discuss the case with anyone. I decided to send them home and require that they be on call to return to the court upon notice. I proposed this novel approach to all the attorneys involved. They agreed to it. I advised each person selected that he or she had been prequalified to serve and would be officially sworn in upon their return to court. Based on my previous experience with capital cases, I surmised that jury selection would last a while. I put my proposal on the record and had each attorney acknowledge agreement. Taylor's appellate counsel filed a brief with the Louisiana Supreme Court claiming I committed a reversible error when I did not sequester jurors according to the Louisiana Code of Criminal Procedure. The Supreme Court said that since defense counsel agreed to this procedure before the selection process began, it waived any error on this point.

Because the delayed sequestration procedure worked so well in the

*Feltus Taylor* case, prosecuting attorney John Sinquefield introduced the idea to the Louisiana District Attorneys Association and proposed a procedural change to the Louisiana Legislature. The legislature amended the Code of Criminal Procedure to allow for a delay in sequestration when the state and defense jointly so move.

We began the guilt phase of the trial, which was straightforward. It was unusual for a defendant to take the stand in his defense and effectively confess his guilt during this phase, which lasted only two days. The second phase, wherein the jury considers the penalty following a conviction, is far more deliberate and intense, as it deals with the question of life or death.

Once a trial gets past the guilt phase, the penalty phase is where the defense attorneys feel the most pressure because they are now trying to save the defendant's life. In the initial part of this phase, the prosecutor presents facts that meet any aggravating circumstances that the law requires a jury to find before they can recommend the death penalty. In the *Taylor* case, the prosecution relied upon four aggravating circumstances: (1) that the defendant was engaged in the perpetration or attempted perpetration of an armed robbery; (2) that the defendant created a risk of death or great bodily harm to more than one person; (3) that the defendant was convicted of a previously unrelated armed robbery; and (4) that the offense was committed in an especially heinous, atrocious, and cruel manner.

During the trial's penalty phase, the prosecution called three witnesses, all family members of the victim, to provide victim impact evidence. Such evidence often humanizes a victim and provides the jury with information about how the crime impacted the victim's survivors.

Defense counsel can offer any mitigating evidence that might sway the jury from imposing the death penalty as a counter to the prosecution's victim impact evidence. In this particular case, the defense called a total of twenty witnesses, including the defendant.

During the defense mitigation portion of the trial, chaos broke out when Taylor's grandmother was called as a mitigation witness against the death penalty. The defendant screamed out loudly and, with all his might, lifted the heavy oak table where he was seated with his counsel and flipped it over, which caused all of the items on top to fly all over the courtroom. The defendant's antics had jurors running from their seats as deputies tackled him, pushing him to the floor. I immediately returned the jury to the jury room until order in the courtroom was regained. All the jurors were visibly shaken by what they had witnessed.

After a two-hour recess, the defendant was brought back into the courtroom so I could determine what was behind his outburst. He said that he had told his attorneys that he did not want his grandmother to testify on his behalf. They called her against his wishes. I explained to him that it was their job to fight for his life, and they had decided that his grandmother should speak to the jury on his behalf if that was what she wanted. I suggested to the defendant to let his attorneys do their job, and I received his assurance that there would be no further outbreaks once the trial resumed.

After the jury returned to their seats, I cautioned them that what they had witnessed in the courtroom should not influence the decision they had to make in this case. Their decision had to be based solely upon the evidence presented from the testimony of witnesses from the witness stand as well as all physical evidence introduced at trial.

The case finally moved to the point of closing arguments, and it then became my duty to charge the jury as to the law that applies to this case. I told them that they were the judges of both the law and the evidence and were required to accept the law given to them by the court.

The jury's deliberation only lasted about five hours, after five days of hearing witnesses during the penalty phase of the trial. There was a knock on the door, and the bailiff advised me that the jury had a verdict. Waiting for the jury's verdict in a death penalty case always produces a lot of anxiety. Once the verdict is returned and announced by the foreman, judges anticipate some form of outburst from the audience and try to be prepared to maintain order in the courtroom. I had directed the deputies in the courtroom to be on alert.

One sign that a verdict will be unfavorable to a defendant is when jurors, upon returning to the courtroom, refuse to make eye contact with the defendant. That was evident in this instance. The foreman informed me that the jury had reached a verdict. I reviewed the verdict sheet and then asked the reporter to read the verdict. It was unanimous. The jury recommended that Feltus Taylor be sentenced to death for the murder of Donna Ponsano, in violation of Louisiana Revised Statute 14:30. Each of the jurors was polled individually as to their vote.

As anticipated, there was a slight outburst in the courtroom, but it was quickly quashed. I instructed the jury to retire to the jury room, telling them that I would be in to speak to them shortly. The defendant took the verdict calmly, as if reconciled to his fate.

When I went into the jury room, there was hardly a dry eye among the women. Coming to a verdict of death was extremely hard on them. I believe the defendant made it a little easier for them when he said he did not blame them if they chose the death penalty in his case. Despite my cautionary warning to the jury, the defendant's courtroom outburst may have also helped seal his fate.

To ensure that I didn't stutter or lose my composure on the day of Taylor's sentencing, I sat down in chambers and scripted a sentencing statement that would be appropriate under the law. In essence, I told the defendant that he had been found guilty of first-degree murder by a jury of his peers and was to die by lethal injection according to the jury's recommendation. I rapped my gavel, adjourned court, and headed off to my chambers for a moment of solitude and reflection. I felt hollow and questioned whether anyone had the right to pass a death sentence upon another human being. I thought about my position on the death penalty and my conflict of conscience. After much reflection, I resolved that I was obliged to impose that sentence in keeping with my oath to uphold the constitution and laws of the State of Louisiana.

As I was the lone African American judge in Baton Rouge, I welcomed Ralph Tyson's and Curtis Calloway's election to the Baton Rouge City Court almost two years after my election to the district court. Ralph was my former law partner, and Curtis was a good friend. Being the only Black judge in the entire parish for almost six years made for a lonesome existence. Carl Stewart, a district court judge in Shreveport, Louisiana, and I were the only two Black judges in Louisiana outside of the New

Orleans metropolitan area. Having Ralph and Curtis join the Baton Rouge judicial ranks proved quite refreshing and provided me with a new source of collaboration.

Like me, Ralph and Curtis ran against white opponents. Demographically they, too, were not supposed to win. But my two successful campaigns for city and district court provided a road map for them to follow. Both ran outstanding campaigns and defied the political pundits by winning their respective elections.

After the Tyson and Calloway elections, Ed Pratt, an African American newspaper reporter for the *Morning Advocate,* wrote an article on August 31, 1989, questioning whether their elections signaled a change in the political climate in Baton Rouge. He said the question started with my election to the Baton Rouge City Court, followed by my election to the Nineteenth Judicial District Court. As to the question of whether my victories and the elections of Tyson and Calloway signaled a change in the political climate in Baton Rouge, I responded by saying that "it was just a glimmer, a flicker of change at best." I was not ready to fully endorse the idea that the winds of change had blown away all of the elements of racial animus that had held Blacks back when pitted against white candidates. It's challenging to run a sophisticated and well-organized campaign without having ample financial resources, which proved to be the stumbling block for most Black candidates.

After analyzing my district court win, Pratt's article quoted Nancy Todd, a national political consultant, who said, "Freddie Pitcher's [last] election was an aberration. . . . The suit [*Clark v. Edwards*] had something to do with it."

Nancy Todd's reference to the *Clark v. Edwards* suit angered me. I felt that she dismissed my qualifications and the hard work it took to win that district court seat. Her subtle implication was that had the lawsuit not existed, I would not have won. When I ran for the city court, there was no *Clark v. Edwards* lawsuit, and I still won.

Another political consultant, Roy Fletcher, was quoted by Pratt as saying: "Freddie Pitcher just did a good job of campaigning; it was no small feat that Pitcher was able to get the majority of the legal community to support him. He had all of the endorsements." How else could I have captured more than forty-three thousand votes and some 52 percent of the votes cast?

❦-❦

The only time candidates get a chance to find out how they are doing is when they face the electorate. On July 27, 1992, however, the *Morning Advocate* newspaper decided to publish performance data on all the judges of the Nineteenth Judicial District Court. The newspaper sent questionnaires to several hundred lawyers asking them to evaluate judges in several different categories. I had been on the district court for nearly four years and was delighted to learn that I was in a virtual tie with Mike McDonald for the top-rated criminal court judge on that court. The article stated:

> State District Judges Mike McDonald and Freddie Pitcher, Jr. are neck and neck as the top-rated criminal court judges in a survey of attorneys about the judiciary in East Baton Rouge Parish. . . .
>
> More than 400 attorneys participated in the survey to rate 26 state, federal and city court judges in five general categories and 30 subcategories. The attorneys used a scale of one to five, with one being the lowest and five the highest. The respondents are anonymous. . . .
>
> Pitcher, a former city judge who has served as a state district judge since 1988, was rated well above the criminal court and overall averages by attorneys who identified themselves as either prosecutors or criminal defense attorneys.
>
> The two groups gave Pitcher the same or similar ratings on many criteria. Both gave him scores above the overall survey average for fair and consistent sentencing practices and clear and complete rulings, for overall integrity and for understanding complex legal issues.
>
> "Innovative and intelligent," one attorney said about Pitcher. . . .

Pitcher's overall scores include ratings above the overall average in every category. He received scores well above the overall average in integrity, impartiality and judicial temperament. He was slightly above the overall average in professional competence and his work ethic was rated highest among the criminal court judges.

Some of Pitcher's highest overall scores are for courtesy to attorneys, courtesy to the public and jurors, being free of arrogance, efficiency in managing his caseload, intelligence and accessibility during working hours.

Pitcher also has overall scores of 4.5 for ruling without sexual bias and 4.1 for ruling without racial or ethnic bias. The criminal court average in those criteria is 4.1 and 4.0, respectively.

"I feel delighted to know that I'm highly thought of by members of the professional bar," Pitcher said. As the parish's first black state district judge, Pitcher said he knew "a lot of eyes were going to be focused on me."

The judge said he has tried to be "the best judge that I could possibly be."

After my election to the district court, I continued honoring requests to speak to elementary, junior high, and senior high school students about the court system and my role as a judge. On one of those engagements, a teacher, Ms. Jones, asked me if I would be willing to come back to speak to a group of Black males in her school about the perils of dropping out of school and its connection to crime and prison. She taught at Prescott Middle School and was concerned about the excessive number of students dropping out of school at this level. I agreed to do so and arranged to come back on a Saturday morning to spend a couple of hours talking with the students about the criminal justice system.

With this engagement locked in, I decided to use my position as a district court judge as a bully pulpit to rally the Black lawyers around our making a coordinated frontal attack on the school-to-prison pipeline. I called a late-afternoon meeting of the Louis A. Martinet Society to talk about how we could help stem the tide of young Black boys and girls getting into the school-to-prison pipeline. At the meeting, I told the group that we had a responsibility to reach out to the kids now instead of seeing them after they are in trouble or on their way to prison. The Martinet members attending the meeting thought this was a great idea and agreed to join me in this presentation. Since the students were coming out on a Saturday, we agreed to provide them with a light continental breakfast and raised a couple of hundred dollars to cover the breakfast cost.

I suggested that we break our presentation into three modules, following a similar program where I was a presenter. The first module dealt with the relationship between education and employment, the second with drugs and crime in the community, and the third with positive self-image and self-esteem. The attorneys volunteered for one of the three modules and developed their presentations before our Saturday meeting. I especially wanted Bonnie Jackson, an assistant public defender at that time, and Tony Clayton, an assistant district attorney, to present in the drug and crime module. I also contacted Larry Smith, deputy commissioner of corrections, for his help in getting a warden at one of the correctional facilities to allow a couple of inmates to participate with us in the program and talk about prison life as a deterrent to crime.

The morning of our presentation rolled around, and everything went off like clockwork. We had more than fifty kids from the seventh, eighth, and ninth grades attending. Several curious parents also showed up. The presentations by the prisoners were particularly impactful as they got the students' attention right off the bat. In our postmortem, we all agreed the program was a success and was something we should continue. From this meeting, the Metropolitan Area Law League (MALL) was formed and developed a partnership with the East Baton Rouge Parish School System to help stem the tide of school dropouts and halt the school-to-prison pipeline.

After a series of meetings between our group and Robert Williams, an assistant superintendent of the East Baton Rouge School System, we put together a plan to meet once a month with at-risk students referred to us as an alternative to being suspended from school for violating a school policy. The students would report to their schools on a Saturday morning, and a school bus would pick them up and bring them downtown to the courthouse to spend a half day with us going through our three modules. Judge Calloway was the liaison for the school system and coordinated with Assistant Superintendent Williams for the students' participation.

I continued in the leadership of MALL until I moved to the First Circuit Court of Appeal. Judge Calloway took over the leadership when I stepped down. What was so refreshing about this interaction with the students was the interest many parents took in our program; they requested that we provide them with some parenting tools for kids who were at risk. With this request, I approached Dr. Clotiel Nelson, a professor in the College of Education at Southern University, to see if she could help us put something together to meet the needs of these parents. Dr. Nelson and Dr. Rose Duhon-Sells, chairman of the College of Education, met the challenge and started meeting with the parents and us when we held our Saturday sessions with the students.

This collaboration between the court system, the school system, Southern University, and the Department of Corrections worked well for several years and helped, we believe, limit the number of those entering the school-to-prison pipeline. Unfortunately, the program began to wane when the leadership of MALL passed from the judges to the attorneys, and it ceased operation after about four years.

# 7

## Moving Up

### *Louisiana First Circuit Court of Appeal*

**A**FTER WINNING THE district court seat, I focused on being the best judge I could be while serving out my term. I hoped my performance would warrant reelection when the time came. I was not looking past the district court seat. But as fate would have it, the *Clark v. Edwards* lawsuit presented an opening for a seat on the Louisiana First Circuit Court of Appeal. Six years into litigation, the suit had made its way through the trial court and invariably headed to the U.S. Fifth Circuit Court of Appeals. The Fifth Circuit would be considering the correctness of Judge John Parker's ruling that the system of electing Louisiana family court, district court, and court of appeal judges violated Section 2 of the Voting Rights Act. Judge Parker had issued a permanent injunction prohibiting the State of Louisiana from holding elections under that system. His ruling meant that no judicial elections could occur until a remedy could be approved to cure the problem.

In an attempt to avoid further federal court action, the Louisiana Legislature drafted a new system of electing judges that created subdistricts. A similar proposal had failed as a constitutional amendment when put before the people in a statewide election on October 7, 1989. The plaintiffs' lawyers proposed the new system. Attorneys Janice Clark and Ernest Johnson were the lead negotiators, joined by State Senator Charles Jones, who was chairman of Louisiana's Legislative Black Caucus.

Because the entire Louisiana judicial system was involved in this lawsuit, it was interesting to sit through the Louisiana District Court Judges Association meetings. Judge Carl Stewart, who is now on the U.S. Fifth Circuit Court of Appeals, and I usually were the only two Black judges attending these meetings. Black judges in New Orleans didn't feel the need to get involved because Black judges there could be elected without resorting to subdistricts. Opposition to settling the lawsuit was extremely high, and many of the judges at these meetings were quite vocal. Carl and I would often be on the opposite side of the majority of the district judges voting on the subject.

East Baton Rouge Parish and the Nineteenth Judicial District plan would have created three new subdistricts, which would have yielded possibly four Black judges and a seat on the Louisiana First Circuit Court of Appeal. My district court seat was to be in the subdistrict. At that time, I was the only Black judge on the Nineteenth Judicial District Court. Of the twelve judges on the First Circuit, none was Black. In a *State-Times* article written by Tuck Thompson on August 30, 1989, I reaffirmed my support for the proposed subdistrict plan, saying: "Judge Parker has spoken. He's given the state an opportunity to fashion a remedy. . . . I am not saying it is the best possible remedy, but it's a good remedy." Thompson also asked me about the possibility of my moving up to the First Circuit Court of Appeal. I responded by saying that such a move would be a logical progression, and it was one that I would not be opposed to making. An elected term on the court of appeal in Louisiana is ten years compared to six on the district court. I was uncertain about moving up to the appellate court, but I realized that I could be forever locked out from a future run if I didn't make a move at the first opportunity.

My colleagues on the district court were divided on the question of subdistricts. Most opposed Judge Parker's ruling but were willing to go along with implementing a subdistrict plan. Tuck Thompson's article quoted Judge L. J. Hymel as saying: "I saw nothing wrong with the old system of electing judges. I am not in agreement with (Parker's) decision at all. I hope it's appealed." Hymel also said that "a new breed of black attorneys here has followed Pitcher's lead and learned how to get white voter support parish-wide. Pitcher's success in elections to city court and later district court is proof that the electoral system would have cured itself." Although I had been successful in the two judicial races I entered, I was not as optimistic as my friend L. J. Hymel about the future chances of the new breed of Black attorneys getting sufficient white support. His observation was partially true, but my success with white voters had a lot to do with relationships I developed over the years when I was an assistant district attorney and special counsel in the Attorney General's Office.

The constitutional amendment was resoundingly defeated by the voters, to the disappointment of all its proponents. The defeat meant that the subdistrict remedy fell back into the hands of Judge Parker, who adopted the proposed judicial remedy and made it a part of his final judgment. The next step in the litigation was to go to the U.S. Fifth Circuit Court of Appeal. Many thought that that court would not be receptive to this voters' rights case, as it had taken on a conservative bent since some of its historic rulings of the 1960s.

At the urging of Janice Clark and on behalf of all plaintiffs in the case, State Senator Charles Jones entered into negotiations with Attorney General Richard Ieyoub to see if an agreement could be reached before a ruling was handed down by the U.S. Fifth Circuit Court of Appeal. Both sides agreed that a negotiated deal would be better than the uncertainty of what might come out of the court. After several weeks of negotiation, the parties settled, effectively ending the six-year-old case. The governor and the attorney general signed off on the agreement in the form of a consent decree that established a new judicial system for electing judges in Louisiana.

As it turned out, the decision to pursue settling was fortuitous because *Lulac v. the State of Texas,* a companion case to *Clark v. Edwards,* continued through the appellate process and was reversed by the U.S. Fifth Circuit. The *Clark* case would indeed have suffered a similar fate had it not been settled.

After *Clark v. Edwards* settled, the newly created subdistrict seat on the Louisiana First Circuit Court of Appeal was back on my radar. I saw it as an opportunity that I couldn't pass up. If not now, and with ten-year terms, it might never be.

On August 19, 1992, the first day of qualifying for all the judicial elections that Judge Parker had enjoined, I filed for the newly created seat on the Louisiana First Circuit Court of Appeal. Qualifying closed on August 22. During that time, I heard several names tossed about as possible opponents. In the end, however, no one filed to run against me for the appellate court judgeship. What a relief! The stress and tension of possibly going through another election dissipated almost immediately after I learned I had no opposition.

After running citywide for a judgeship on the Baton Rouge City Court and parish-wide for the Nineteenth Judicial District Court, I was thrilled to move up another level in the court system in Louisiana—this time in a walk, not a run.

Though the election occurred in October, I was not due to assume my seat on the court of appeal until January 1, 1993. I went over to speak with my good friend and judicial mentor Judge Melvin Shortess. After my election to the Baton Rouge City Court, Judge Shortess was there for me whenever I had questions concerning any aspect of the judicial process. As I would be joining him as a colleague on the First Circuit, his advice and counsel were invaluable as I prepared to make this move.

I needed to hone my writing skills. I didn't want it said that my law clerks wrote all of my opinions. I found two legal writing seminars to help me quickly perfect my writing skills. They were practically back-to-back, but I thought it important enough to attend both.

The First Circuit Court of Appeal was now located in a commercial building on Acadian Thruway at Bawell Street. Bawell ran from Acadian to College Drive and cut through Valley Park, my old neighborhood. When I was growing up in Valley Park, Bawell dead-ended about three hundred yards before reaching Acadian. At my swearing-in ceremony, I told the audience how significant it was to stand in this particular building that day. As a youngster growing up in Valley Park, I told them, I would have to go back to Valley Street, turn right onto Valley, make another right turn on Perkins, and go down to Acadian Thruway, a total distance of about three miles. Hopefully, because of the barriers we have broken down, young Black boys and girls will never again have to travel three miles to go three hundred yards. My comment received rousing applause from the audience as the overwhelming crowd of Black folks understood what I meant with this metaphor. My election marked another first for African Americans in East Baton Rouge Parish, as well as the sixteen parishes that fell within the jurisdiction of the Louisiana First Circuit Court of Appeal.

I was assigned to sit on a three-judge panel with two judges who, I soon learned, had a deep dislike for one another. After oral arguments, the judges on a three-judge panel traditionally get together and discuss the cases before them that day. Sometimes they would confer over lunch. Because of the bad relations between these two judges, I did not experience such collegiality. Though I got along well with each of my fellow judges when we met one-on-one, we never sat together to discuss our joint cases. I conducted a lot of "shuttle diplomacy" between the two. Chief Judge Morris Lottinger dropped by my office one day and invited me to lunch. He wanted to know how things were going and whether there was anything he could do to help me. He apologized for assigning me to sit with two men who were at odds with one another. Their antipathy began when one of the judges supported Kitty Kimball for the Louisiana Supreme Court while the other ran against her for the same seat. Justice Kimball won, but collegiality lost. Court business was conducted by interoffice memorandums and through their law clerks' communication.

One of the most challenging cases I faced in my initial assignment on the court involved an appeal of a suit to recover benefits under a life insurance policy. The lawsuit, *Louisiana Commercial Bank et al., Plaintiffs, v. Georgia International Life Insurance Company et al., Defendants,* was of particular interest because it involved a question of insurance coverage for Noel "Butch" Baum, a high-profile insurance company executive and candidate for governor. Baum, a pilot, died in a peculiar plane crash. He had a million-dollar insurance policy through Georgia International Life Insurance Company. His policy contained an aviation exclusion clause, which turned out to be the flashpoint of the controversy.

I was the writing judge on the case, which meant that I had to read the briefs, research the law, and write the opinion. A second judge, called the backup judge, is assigned to read the briefs and research the law but not write. The third judge on the panel would read the briefs but is not obliged to research or write. I decided to visit the backup judge to discuss the issues in the case and get his thoughts on the matter. He provided no new insight and instead was waiting for me and my report on the appeal. I realized then that I was on my own, and the only help I was going to get was within the four corners of my office.

After thoroughly researching the case, I wrote an opinion reversing the trial court's judgment. The third judge on the panel joined the opinion. The backup judge concurred and provided written reasons. The Louisiana Supreme Court denied writs in the case, bolstering my confidence.

I had to work hard to reacclimate myself to the civil side of the law after spending practically all of my district court tenure handling criminal cases. I was determined to meet the challenge, however. After sitting through several cycles of oral argument and staying up late to research the law, I became more and more comfortable as an appellate court judge. The help and exceptional assistance of my two law clerks, Kathy Flynn Simino and Jacquelyn Watts, made it possible for me to reach a comfort level I came to enjoy. Although I typed my own opinions, Carolyn Ricks, my secretary since I began to practice law, contributed significantly to our office operations and ensured we stayed on task vis-à-vis deadlines, opinions, and writ duty assignments.

It was somewhat unsettling for me to find the First Circuit devoid of African Americans, except for Mr. Willie Vaughn, the court's in-house mailman. Carolyn Ricks, Jacquelyn Watts, and I increased the court's diversity to four. In 1993, a court that serviced a sixteen-parish jurisdiction should have had a more diverse support staff. I questioned why we didn't have Blacks working in the clerk of court's office and why there were no Black attorneys on central staff. When I raised the question at a meeting, one of the judges who had served on the court for many years asked me why I thought I, the lone Black judge, could change how the First Circuit did things. I explained to him that I had the entire Legislative Black Caucus behind me, and they were interested in having our courts reflect our community. The judge told me that the Black Caucus didn't have any authority over judges. I pointed out that the court had to go to the legislature for support and salary increases. My admonition angered him, and he stomped out of the room.

A couple of days later, Chief Judge Lottinger assured me that he was sensitive to my concerns, and efforts were underway to make some changes. A Black former deputy sheriff was added to the court's security staff, and then a young Black woman was hired as a clerical worker in the clerk's office. Those two changes might not have been much, but it was a start. After Jacquelyn Watts's clerkship ended, I hired Annie Gunn, followed by Valerie Blunt, as law clerks to keep the diversity employment trend going.

## Associate Justice Ad Hoc on the Louisiana Supreme Court

On March 14, 1996, Chief Justice Pascal Calogero, Justice Walter Marcus, and Justice Bernette Johnson voluntarily recused themselves in *Clement F. Perschall, Jr. v. The State of Louisiana*. The case challenged the election of two of the Louisiana Supreme Court's seven justices from a single district that included Orleans Parish. The issue at hand involved the constitutionality of a statute adopted to resolve a federal voting rights case.

I got a call from Justice Kitty Kimball, for whom I clerked at the Attorney General's Office when I was in law school, who asked me to accept an appointment to the supreme court as an associate justice ad hoc on the *Perschall* case. I agreed without hesitation. Such an appointment was indeed an honor. Although I would serve only for the *Perschall* case, it was an important matter and highly consequential. The appointment would also mean that I would have sat as a judge at every level of the Louisiana court system—city, district, court of appeal, and now the supreme court. Although I was not breaking new ground here, this was a personal achievement. I would be joining Dr. Jesse Stone and Judge Felicia Toney Williams as the only African Americans outside of Justices Bernette Johnson and Revius Ortique Jr. to have had the honor of serving on the Louisiana Supreme Court. I had come a long way from sitting on the bench in front of Owens Grocery.

The *Perschall* case revolved around the constitutionality of Act 512 of the 1992 Louisiana legislative session. Act 512 was adopted to resolve *Chisom v. Edwards*, a federal voting rights case that challenged the election of two of the supreme court's seven justices from a single district that included Orleans Parish. Under a consent judgment between the parties, Act 512 created an additional seat on the Fourth Court of Appeal. The judge elected to that seat would be assigned to the supreme court as a justice.

After a briefing on the issues by the parties, the *Perschall* case was ready for oral argument. Even though I had been a judge for thirteen years at this point, it was still an incredible feeling to walk into a courtroom and take a seat beside the justices of the Louisiana Supreme Court. My mind flashed back to the one case I argued before the supreme court when I was a young attorney with the DA's Office. I was in awe as I looked up at the justices from my podium. Now I was in awe sitting on this bench looking down at the litigants.

A draft of the proposed *Perschall* opinion was circulated among the justices for a vote to join, concur, or dissent. The court's final opinion found that Act 512 was unconstitutional in its entirety but recognized that its operational effect would remain intact. The court was to continue to function as a de jure (legal) court under the *Chisom* consent judgment, deferring a final determination to the jurisdiction of the U.S. District Court for the Eastern District of Louisiana. I was struck by the decision of the majority, especially given how the oral arguments had gone. Justice Kimball, the opinion's author, was harshly criticized in the press for her aggressive questioning of Perschall regarding his standing to bring the lawsuit in the first place. I also had questions about Perschall's standing and knew from the outset that I was opposed to his attack on the constitutionality of Act 512. I assumed that I would be joined in dissent by at least one other justice but found myself as the lone dissenter.

My dissent was short. I noted that I did not believe that Act 512 effectively imposed the eighth justice on the supreme court. Section 312.4 did nothing more than establish an additional judgeship for the Fourth Circuit Court of Appeal, increasing the number of judges on that court to thirteen. Assigning a judge from the Fourth Circuit to the Supreme Court for seven years was well within the court's purview.

The *Perschall* case made its way to the U.S. Court of Appeals for the Fifth Circuit. The judges there dismissed Perschall's case for his lack of standing. I felt that the Fifth Circuit's resolution was how the Louisiana Supreme Court should have resolved the case and took solace in knowing that I was correct in my belief that Perschall did not have standing to bring his lawsuit.

## Honorary African Chief

While serving on the First Circuit Court of Appeal, I had the opportunity to join a delegation of several Southern faculty members traveling to Nigeria as part of the United States Information Agency's Democracy in Africa program. It was a joint undertaking by the University of Lagos Law School and the Southern University Law Center to foster an exchange of ideas and information as Nigeria and the United States improved their respective democratic processes. During a series of seminars held from April 6 through April 11, 1995, we presented papers at the University of Lagos, Obafemi Awolowo University, and the University of Ibadan. Our goal was to raise thought-provoking ideas about the democratic process. I made two presentations at each seminar. One was entitled "An Overview of the American Jury Trial System," and the other was "Sentencing Guidelines: A Questionable Alternative to Discretion." The project's central theme was "Human, Civil, and Political Rights," which drew large audiences that included university lecturers, attorneys, representatives of most Nigerian human rights organizations, diplomats, journalists, students, and the general public.

When we landed in Lagos on April 4, 1995, a person who introduced himself as our "expediter" met us and ushered us through customs. Without him, we would have been required to pay the customary "dash," or bribe, to customs agents to ensure we were reunited with our luggage.

Once the expediter helped us get our bags, we proceeded to a van waiting to take us to the University of Lagos, where we would be staying the first few days of our trip. Before our van could leave, special agents of the Nigerian government blocked our departure. One of the agents asked to see our identification and explain why we had come to Nigeria. We told him that we were from the United States and had come to participate in a joint program between Lagos University and the Southern University Law School. The purpose was to discuss democracy in Africa and America. We were required to hand over copies of the papers we were to present at the conference.

Our host, Dean Akintunde O. Obilade, was visibly shaken by the turn of events, which of course caused us great concern. One agent got into the van with us and proceeded to accompany us everywhere we went during our entire stay in Nigeria.

We learned that our host had promoted our team as human rights activists, which would have been anathema to General Sani Abacha, the Nigerian head of state, who himself stood accused of numerous human rights violations. General Abacha had seized control of the government in a military coup and decreed that he had absolute power to detain anyone for up to three months without a trial. The government would not allow foreigners to disparage or undermine General Abacha or his government. Our safety had become somewhat tenuous due to how our host had characterized our lectures. We were anxious to conclude our business and board our plane unscathed when our visit to Nigeria ended on April 14.

Dr. Gloria Braxton, the director of the Center of International Development Programs at Southern University and co-director of the Democracy in Africa project, and Akintunde O. Obilade, the dean and professor of law at Lagos University, addressed the human rights aspect of our seminars. I was to present my paper on the American jury trial system, followed by Professor Jacqueline Nash. She was to address "The Face of Poverty in Louisiana and the Role of Legal Services." Professor Russell Jones then would discuss the Fourth Amendment and unlawful searches and seizures. When I finished making my presentation, I was inundated with numerous questions about the O. J. Simpson and Rodney King trials, leaving no time for my colleagues to deliver their papers. Millions of Nigerians had learned of both cases from cable news networks, and they questioned whether the outcome of those cases justified the harsh criticism of the jury trial system, which was adopted and then abandoned in Nigeria after two years. The seminar directors decided that my co-presenters would present their papers at our next two stops before I spoke.

An unexpected honor occurred when one of the Nigerian law professors invited us to the township of Idoko in Osun State, where he grew up. His uncle was the oba (king) there. Before our trip to Idoko, the professor had a tailor come to our quarters and measure Dr. Braxton and me for traditional Nigerian attire to wear at a special ceremony. He told us that the ceremony would be presided over by the oba himself. Our outfits were completed in one day and were fit for royalty. The ceremony took place in a building equivalent to a town hall in the United States. Many townspeople attended. There was a lot of singing and dancing before the oba motioned for Dr. Braxton and me to come forward and kneel. Then he gave a rousing ceremonial colloquy, which neither of us understood. Throughout it all, we remained kneeling on the floor. When the oba finished, he declared we were now honorary African chiefs. I was titled "Chief Bamofin" of Idoko-Ilesa, Nigeria, which translates to "one learned in the law" in recognition of my judgeship on the Louisiana First Circuit Court of Appeal.

Before leaving Nigeria, our group was fortunate to meet Bishop Desmond Tutu, who was visiting Walter C. Carrington, the U.S. ambassador to Nigeria, at the same time we were.

# 8

## Postjudicial Years and New Heights in Academia

**A**FTER FOUR AND a half years on the First Circuit Court of Appeal, I had settled into the routine of an appellate court judge. What loomed on the home front were my wife's and daughter's dreams, desires, and aspirations. Harriet had long wanted to pursue a doctorate in her area of speech pathology or special education. Having received her bachelor's degree in music from Howard University, Kyla was anxious to pursue a master of music degree at the University of South Carolina. She had been awarded an assistantship in their opera theater program. The big question for me was whether my family could achieve its goals on the salary of an appellate court judge. After analyzing the numbers, it became clear the answer was no. I decided that Harriet and Kyla should not have to defer their dreams any longer. It was time for me to help my girls achieve them.

A good friend and ardent supporter suggested that I was in a prime position to move into the private sector as a partner with one of the major law firms. Compensation in these firms far exceeded what I was making as an appellate court judge. He indicated that his old firm was interested in me joining them as a partner and offered to arrange a meeting with the managing partner if and when I was ready. I decided to call my friend Reuben Anderson, the first Black person to serve on the Mississippi Supreme Court, who was now a partner at a large law firm, to get insight on moving from the judiciary into the practice.

I first met Reuben when he was a law student at Southern University while I was an undergraduate. After his freshman year, Reuben transferred to the University of Mississippi School of Law. He was elected to the supreme court following his appointment to that court by the governor. Our paths crossed again when we were both invited to attend Nelson Mandela's address to a joint session of Congress on June 26, 1990. At that time, Reuben told me that he was leaving his seat on the Mississippi Supreme Court for a partnership with a major law firm. As I was about to enter into discussions with a firm in Baton Rouge, I wanted to know what it was like moving into the private sector after years on the bench. Reuben wanted to know what law firm I was considering and asked me not to do anything before his firm spoke to me. Two days later, Alston Johnson, the managing partner of the Baton Rouge office of Phelps Dunbar, LLP, called to discuss my joining that law firm. And after a whirlwind two-week courtship, which included two other law firms making overtures to me, I decided to leave the bench and accept a partnership at Phelps Dunbar. When I explained this new venture to Harriet and Kyla, they also agreed it was the right family decision.

I called a press conference to announce my decision to leave the bench after nearly fifteen years of combined judicial service and to reveal my private-sector plans. I explained that the reason I ran for a judgeship in 1983 was no longer relevant in 1997. I had run to open up the judiciary to Blacks in Baton Rouge. Where once there was just one, now nine Black judges served in East Baton Rouge Parish. With my new venture, I would be the first African American partner in the Baton Rouge office of Phelps Dunbar, a regional law firm of about 240 lawyers at the time. Because my seat on the First Circuit was part of the *Clark v. Edwards* settlement, my leaving the bench would not jeopardize a subdistrict seat.

On May 15, 1996, Harriet received her doctor of education degree (Ed.D) from Nova Southeastern University, and Kyla received a master's degree in opera theater from the University of South Carolina in July 1996. Kyla was later awarded a fellowship from LSU to pursue a doctorate in musical arts (DMA), which she received in June 2007. The decision to step down from the court of appeal not only opened a new door for me in the private sector but also solidified new opportunities for both Harriet and Kyla.

### Appointed Chancellor of the Southern University Law Center

One of the most gratifying achievements of my entire career as a lawyer, aside from my judicial service, was my selection as chancellor of the Southern University Law Center, my alma mater. Encouraged by a number of my fellow alumni, I applied for the position when it appeared that the Southern University Board of Supervisors could not agree on a leader after the departure of Chancellor B. K. Agnihotri, the Law Center's leader for twenty-seven years. He resigned the chancellorship to become the ambassador-at-large for the government of India, his native country.

Chancellor Agnihotri and I developed a strong relationship over the years, and on several occasions he suggested that I succeed him as the Law Center's chancellor. During the search for the new Law Center chancellor, I learned that Governor Mike Foster phoned Ambassador Agnihotri to get his thoughts on who the next chancellor should be. I was honored to have him recommend me to Governor Foster as the person who should succeed him. The governor told Agnihotri that he didn't know me but would like to meet me.

While Agnihotri was chancellor, Governor Foster became a part-time law student at the Southern University Law Center. It appeared he was giving a wink and nod to the Southern University Board of Supervisors, who all were appointed by him, on who should or should not be the next chancellor of the Southern University Law Center. At the suggestion of Ambassador Agnihotri, I was invited to have lunch with the governor, a meeting that went exceptionally well. He told me during the lunch that he didn't want to see a politician take the helm of the Law Center. I assured him I was not a politician. I had merely used the political process to get elected to my judgeships. Once I became a judge, I exited the political game.

I also met with Dr. Leon Tarver for the sole purpose of receiving assurance that he was not supporting someone else in the race. We had a pretty good relationship dating back to when he was the secretary of the

Louisiana Department of Urban and Community Affairs, and I served briefly as its attorney. He assured me that he was not and that the search protocol would be fair and just for all applicants for the chancellor's position. After those meetings, I continued in the search, being interviewed by law students, alumni, faculty, and the Board of Supervisors. On November 15, 2002, I was unanimously appointed chancellor of the Southern University Law Center by the Southern University Board of Supervisors.

At the time of my appointment, the Law Center faced many challenges. After being under scrutiny for more than two years, it finally passed its last American Bar Association (ABA) accreditation sabbatical review. The ABA site visit team raised several concerns about the Law Center's sustained viability and noted weaknesses in its overall legal education program. Because of Southern's consistently low bar passage rate, I was concerned that the Law Center's legal education program was not rigorous enough to prepare our graduates for admission to the bar.

The Law Center's transformation started with our making a case for increased funding from the legislature and a tuition increase. Next, we sought to improve the in-house bar review program and expand our legal writing faculty from two to six to help improve our bar exam passage rate. Then we got approval from the ABA to establish a part-time evening division of the Law Center. Next, we gained approval for and initiated a study abroad program in London, England, that thrived for over a decade, surviving the bus and train terrorist attack in the summer of 2005. We also significantly improved our fundraising, concentrating on endowed professorships, which increased from three to ten—valued at $1 million total. Concurrently, we finished raising funds through federal sources to construct a long-planned building addition that carried a price tag of $14 million. The addition was completed in 2008 and added three new classrooms, expanded library space, and new faculty office space.

"Moving to New Heights of Excellence" helped energize the faculty, staff, students, and alumni to work collectively toward goals that many once believed were impossible for the Southern University Law Center to achieve. One of these was to become a full member of the Association of American Law Schools (AALS), which I announced as an objective at the very outset of my tenure as chancellor. Not only was teaching excellence a core value of AALS but so was research and the production of faculty scholarship. Unfortunately, many thought that the scholarship part was unachievable since only about 20 percent of the faculty had real scholarship agendas. I believe that faculty scholarship informs and improves the quality of teaching and thought it would help move Southern from being a good law school to being an excellent law school. Several faculty members bought into the idea at the very outset and joined in to make it happen. Accordingly, our mission was to meet the faculty scholarship requirement for full membership in AALS by generating three streams of scholarship: first, by hiring new faculty members working toward tenure; second, by encouraging faculty members to seek research grants for the summer; and third, by encouraging research by faculty members holding endowed professorships who wished to retain their professorship. All of these scholarship streams required new sources of revenue, which we achieved through legislative budget increases, fundraising from alumni and friends, and a slight increase in the law school's tuition.

At its annual meeting in San Francisco in January 2010, the Association of American Law Schools recognized the Southern University Law Center as a full member. The core values of quality teaching and scholarship had been met by nearly 80 percent of the Law Center's faculty. At that meeting, a retired law school dean who had served on an ABA site evaluation team for Southern's reaccreditation told me he was amazed that the Southern Law Center had risen to heights he never thought achievable. He congratulated the law school on becoming a full AALS member, calling it a remarkable feat.

The AALS membership and my many other achievements accomplished en route to becoming a judge and law school chancellor happened against the odds, as when I was growing up, Black kids were discouraged from setting their goals too high. I learned along the way that naysayers can trap you into believing that there is no way out or no way up from your current situation. But with belief in your God-given abilities, you can achieve anything you set your mind to attain. There may be zigs and zags along the way, but if you don't take your eye off your goal and never give up, anything is possible.

I think about the time I spent sitting on the bench in front of Owens Grocery store, not knowing what my future held, and marvel at what I have been able to accomplish. Never did I envision that I would be elected to a judgeship three times over. Nor did I imagine serving as an associate justice ad hoc on the Louisiana Supreme Court, becoming a partner in a major law firm, or being named chancellor of a law school. Most of the "boys on the bench" would have been thrilled with a trip to New Orleans. To think I would be making multiple trips to teach and lecture at law schools in Europe, Africa, and Asia was out of the question. On one of my trips to the Republic of Turkey, I received an honorary doctor of law degree from Siirt University, an honor unimaginable during my days on the neighborhood bench. None of these things were on my radar screen growing up. However, I chose not to let the fog of the segregated society in which I grew up dictate the chapters in my life. I stepped outside of my comfort zone and developed the fortitude to forge relationships through jobs and social networking that created opportunities for me to achieve my eventual goal of becoming a judge. God opened doors, and I walked through them.

This memoir is my story, one that I am grateful to tell. I tell it to encourage other young people to dream big, work hard, and never give up! I was able to take a journey that led me from the neighborhood bench to the bar as a lawyer, and to the bench as a judge, and to points beyond—making history and experiencing a world I never thought I would see.

# Afterword

THIS MEMOIR WOULD not be complete without giving a shout-out to the National Bar Association, Inc. (NBA). I was introduced to the NBA in 1972 as a second-year law student and president of the Student Bar Association at Southern University Law School, when I attended its convention in Atlanta, Georgia. I was thoroughly impressed with the gathering of Black lawyers from all over the country, many with star-studded and national credentials, who inspired me to be the best that I could be. As I noted earlier, several attorneys and judges accepted my invitation to come to Southern and participate in our Law Week program at their own expense. Giving back and community building are what I saw in the NBA membership, and it was this kind of unselfishness that I encountered at this convention. I grew to understand the words of Charles Hamilton Houston, late dean of the Howard University Law School and the NAACP's first special counsel, who said, "A lawyer is either a social engineer or a parasite on society." I endeavored to be the former and attended all but five NBA conventions from the year of my admission to the bar in 1973 to the year I stepped down as the chancellor of the Southern University Law Center in 2015.

Attending the NBA convention every year served as a great motivator and gave me the fuel to gird up and go back into the fight for justice for my clients. Every year the convention was in a different city, and attending always proved to be an expensive proposition. My family and I traveled all over the United States and Canada attending the conventions. But the networking opportunities; exposure to high-caliber lawyers like my Omega Psi Phi and Sigma Pi Phi fraternity brothers Fred Gray (attorney for Rosa Parks and Dr. Martin Luther King) and Ben Crump; Willie Gary; and Johnnie Cochran, lawyers who looked like me; and the continuing education programs were well worth it. I became friends with lawyers from all over the United States, which resulted in client referrals and legal fees that more than took care of the cost of attending the affair. After my election to the bench, joining the National Bar Judicial Council proved to be another bonus as it brought me into contact with a cadre of Black judges who were sitting at the pinnacle of the profession, such as Justice Thurgood Marshall and federal judges Spottswood Robinson, Wade McCree, Damon Keith, and Leon Higginbotham.

I would sometimes be asked why I chose to attend the NBA convention over that of the ABA, which is the larger and premier bar association in the country. I often replied that I am a member of both, but I attend the NBA convention because it's like attending a family meeting. There are things you talk about among family members that you don't talk about among strangers. Challenging the system of discrimination and racial prejudice in the United States was still foremost on the agenda of the NBA, and I wanted to find my niche in that fight. I recall hearing then U.S. District Court Judge Alcee Hastings, in a speech he delivered in Seattle, Washington, tell the audience of how a young law student said to him that he wished he could have been around to help him and other civil rights pioneers fight some of the early civil rights battles. Judge Hastings said he told the young man that what he needed to do was to prepare himself to be the best lawyer he could be, because it was inevitable that some of those same battles were going to have to be fought all over again. Judge Hastings, who later became Congressman Hastings, was quite prophetic, and it's a message I have shared with my students in my role of law professor. Today, in 2021, the fight for voting rights is still raging all over the country, mirroring the 1960s. To help with that fight, I helped revitalize a Civil Rights Institute at the Southern University Law Center, renaming it in honor of former dean Louis Berry, a Louisiana civil rights hero.

The NBA wasn't just all about the lawyers. Harriet became active in the women's auxiliary, known initially as the Barristers' Wives. The group later incorporated into a separate body under the name of the Bench and Bar Spouses of the National Bar Association. She first became president of the local chapter in Baton Rouge, which gave her a voice at the national level, and eventually she worked her way up to become its national president. Although I was a judge on the Louisiana First Circuit Court of Appeal, when attending the NBA conventions, I was introduced as Harriet's husband.

In 2014, I was honored to be inducted into the National Bar Association's Hall of Fame.

# ACKNOWLEDGMENTS

After my election to the Louisiana First Circuit Court of Appeal, I thought about writing a piece about Black lawyers ascending to the judiciary in Louisiana. I asked Marjorie McKeithen, granddaughter of former governor John J. McKeithen, to arrange a meeting with her grandfather as I wanted to find out from him what had led to his appointing Israel Augustine Jr. as the first Black judge in Louisiana. After I met with the governor and started to write, the weight and intensity of the caseload on the First Circuit caused me to put the project on hold.

I joined Phelps Dunbar, LLP, some years later, and through many conversations with Alston Johnson, the managing partner of the Baton Rouge office, the idea of writing something about Black judges resurfaced. Alston suggested that I write a memoir about my own journey into the judiciary, which he thought was a compelling story in its own right, instead of writing about Blacks in the judiciary globally. He shared a copy of his own memoir, which he had written for his family. The idea pricked my fancy but again got put on the back burner. I left Phelps after some six years and spent twelve and a half years as chancellor of the Southern University Law Center, without thinking much about writing my memoir.

When I returned to Phelps Dunbar in 2016 as a senior partner, Alston Johnson asked me, "Where are you on the book?" I was kind of embarrassed to reply, "Not very far." Fast-forward to March 2020 and the onset of the COVID pandemic, which pretty much forced me to stay home like most folks at the time. I sat down at my computer and again began to take a serious look at writing something about my journey from the bench in front of Owens Grocery in my old neighborhood of Valley Park to the bench as an elected judge on three different courts in Louisiana.

Every day for over a year, I began to write, recounting vignettes of the story that I share in this memoir. Writing, rewriting, and researching became an obsession.

I owe a lot of thanks to my darling wife, Harriet, for having squirreled away newspaper articles from as far back as 1975, when I was an assistant district attorney. If there was an article with my name in it, Harriet had it. So when I started writing and gathering material, she went into storage and pulled out two boxes filled with newspaper articles and photos and old campaign memorabilia. This wealth of information and history sitting in those two boxes made writing this memoir a lot easier than delving into the archives of the *Morning Advocate* and *State-Times* newspapers.

I thank Alston Johnson for urging me to share my story and for editing the first couple of chapters. As I got deeper into writing, I turned to Rachel Emanuel to read and edit my early drafts of my manuscript. I also thank her for recommending Ayan Rubin as my developmental editor, who helped me to carry this writing project to the finish line. Ayan was a real taskmaster. After reading the first one hundred pages, she suggested that I go back and rewrite the first three chapters. Having to rewrite three chapters was a bummer. But I sucked it up and followed her advice, and I ended up with a far better product. We debated how to say certain things throughout the writing and editing process, with her winning out most of the time.

Others who contributed to helping me get to the finish line by reading parts of my manuscript and/or providing information, encouragement, and editorial suggestions were my daughter, Dr. Kyla Dean Pitcher; my sister and brothers Juanita Winfield and Larry Wayne and Glynn Pitcher; my son, Hillary Comeaux; friends and supporters Betty Banks Morgan, Ruth Wesley, Ollie and Georgia Brown, Charles "Chick" Moore, Ed Walters, Richard Matheny, Kathy Flynn Simino, Cynthia Owens Green, Almenia Freeman Warren, Elisa Stephens, Steve Jarreau, Drs. Thomas Durant, Carolyn Collins, and Press Robinson.

I am truly thankful for all the help that I have received over the years from so many people, who helped to inspire me along the way.

# INDEX

Owens, Donald Ray, 14
Owens, Emma, 13
Owens Grocery and Market, 13–14

Parker, John, 148, 151
Patterson, Mike, 82, 113
Patterson Moot Court Competition, 40–41
Pearson, Roger, 95
Pearson, "Skinny," 94
Perez, Lennie, 53, 84, 113, 120
Pero, Leroy, 84–85
Phelps Dunbar LLP, 160
Pillow, Rosemary, 110
Piper, Frederick, 8
Pitcher, Alex, Jr., 18–20, 36, 52, 73–74; as
    president of the San Francisco Bay Area
    NAACP, 19
Pitcher, Alex, Sr., 19
Pitcher, Emanuel, 15
Pitcher, Eugene "Gene," 17
Pitcher, Freddie, Jr., 1–3; childhood friends
    of (Mason and Henry), 8–9; childhood
    in Valley Park, 5–6, 8–9; enjoyment
    in speaking to students, 96–97; as an
    honorary African chief, 156–58; marriage
    to Harriet, 30; racial segregation and
    discrimination faced by, 14–15; speaking
    engagements of, 145–46; trip to Paris with
    Harriet, 32; work at Southdowns Barber
    Shop, 17; work as a caddy at the Westdale
    Country Club, 16–17
—college education (undergraduate):
    architectural studies of, 17–18; graduation
    from Southern University with a degree
    in political science, 23–24; at Southern
    University, 17–18; summer work-study
    program sponsored by Yale University and
    Community Progress, Inc. (CPI), 20–22
—early professional career: assistant
    director and later acting director of
    the Neighborhood Service Center
    Systems for CAI, 32–35; at Community
    Advancement, Inc. (CAI), 24–26; at the

In-School Neighborhood Youth Corps
    (NYC), 26–27; at Manpower, Inc., 32, 33;
    at the Rumor Center, 38–39; at the U.S.
    Department of Interior's Reclamation
    Bureau (a Job Corps program), 23–24, 26
—election to the Baton Rouge City Court:
    building of a campaign team for the
    election run, 77–84; campaign for the
    Baton Rouge City Court, 66–72, 75–77;
    countdown to election day, 88–89;
    election day results (victory), 89–92; and
    get-out-the-vote (GOTV) plans for, 83–84,
    90; newspaper endorsements for, 87–88;
    support of the Black church during, 72–74;
    support of Harriet during, 67–68, 77;
    support of local attorneys during, 69–70;
    time spent at and decisions made as the
    elected Baton Rouge City Court judge,
    92–96
—election to the Nineteenth Judicial District
    Court: building of a campaign team for
    the election run, 113–18; campaign strategy
    for the election, 119–21, 122, 143–44;
    election day results (victory), 126–28;
    get-out-the-vote (GOTV) operation
    during, 124, 125; importance of Baker,
    Zachary, and Central precincts in, 115–16;
    investiture ceremony after the election
    victory, 127; and the letter to the Baton
    Rouge Bar Association, 120; preparations
    for the election, 112–13; success of as
    Nineteenth Judicial District Court judge,
    144–45; general, 110–11, 144
—elementary, middle, and high school
    education: at Bayou Boys State, 9–10; high
    school football career, 9, 10; lack of career
    choices offered by high school guidance
    counselors, 10; at McKinley Junior High
    School, 6; at McKinley Senior High
    School, 9, 15; at Perkins Road Elementary
    School, 7; problems with another
    student during high school and possible
    expulsion, 10–11